Child in
the Wilderness

This book has been authored by and published under the supervision of the Living ECK Master, Sri Harold Klemp. It is the Word of ECK.

Child in the Wilderness

Harold Klemp

ECKANKAR
Minneapolis, MN

Child in the Wilderness

Copyright © 1989 ECKANKAR

The terms ECKANKAR, ECK, EK, MAHANTA, SOUL TRAVEL, and VAIRAGI, among others, are trademarks of ECKANKAR, P.O. Box 27300, Minneapolis, MN 55427 U.S.A.

Printed in U.S.A.
Library of Congress Catalog Card Number: 89-080105

Cover design by Lois Stanfield
Cover illustration by Susan Sarback
Illustrations by Fraser MacDonald
Back cover photo by Robert Huntley

To Joan

"The Master is the guide, for the chela starts out in a wilderness and must be carried out into the calm of the spiritual worlds."

— *The Shariyat-Ki-Sugmad,* Book One

Contents

Introduction

This book is about God-Realization and the myths that surround the highest state of spiritual realization known to mankind. The first and greatest illusion is that once God-Realization is attained, then the battle for higher consciousness is forever won. This, however, oversimplifies things.

It had often puzzled me while reading *The Tiger's Fang* by Paul Twitchell how he could have reached God-Realization and yet been so painfully lacking in worldly wisdom for years to come. Then, by the grace of God, known in ECKANKAR as the SUGMAD, the initiation of God Consciousness was bestowed upon me. First-hand, I thus knew the agony, torture, yet bliss of God's love. This account is given in chapter 14, "The Experience of God."

The hard part came *after* God-Realization. Now I had to return to the problems of life and confront them. The specter of God's haunting love was always with me, but I found it was a highly personal state of being. No one else could share it. The Secret of the Ages had been given to me, but there was no way to tell anyone of it. It carried me beyond the pleasant cooing of belief and faith, thrusting me into a brilliant world of light shorn of all illusion.

The brightest realization of all was that no one could save me from anything. Not lost, how could I be saved? No longer could I fool myself that someone else might appease the burden of my mistakes through a propitious atonement. The reason was simple: Soul is created out of the substance of God and cannot be eternally lost. No savior could shoulder my burdens, for God-Realization brought with it a full responsibility for everything I ever set into motion.

As mentioned above, God-Realization is surrounded by illusion. This created a problem in trying to arrange an order of chapters for this book. Logically, a writer starts small and ends big: he starts in slavery and ends with spiritual freedom.

While this principle is indeed true, the general understanding of people about life before and after God-Realization is at fault. We imagine that hardship precedes the God state and complete serenity follows after. Fortunately, life has more dimensions than that, for it requires all beings to continually reach for the stars. As I learned for myself, there is always another step in consciousness, always a higher heaven to attain.

In writing this book about God-Realization, I might have been expected to start with all the experiences that displayed my ignorance of spiritual reality. Then, in a single blinding moment, dark ignorance would be driven out and replaced by an experience of complete spiritual illumination. And it was, but not in the way one might suppose. The heart of this book is thus not the experience of God alone, but also the narrative that precedes and follows the experience. It shows how I had to come to terms with this unexcelled state of God Awareness in my everyday life.

Child in the Wilderness is the story of how I resolved the paradox of God-Realization in a world that at face value is much less than a spiritual garden. Tucked away in the hidden places of this book are clues as to how you too may reach the glories of God. It is up to you to separate the bare threads of illusion from the golden ones of truth.

Now, come with me on my journey.

"Don't you suppose that God's love can transcend mankind's divisions of time, religion, or circumstance?" the man asked.

1

Was This an ECK Master?

The road to God-Realization may be a difficult one indeed, but there is help for all who love God so dearly as life itself.

This book begins with my first awareness of that help. It came during my senior year in the high school department of a Lutheran preministerial college, when the troubles of my little world seemed ready to crush me. But a stranger appeared, to help me sort through them. Ten years later, in a wholly new setting, he came again: this time to head me more directly toward ECK—the Holy Spirit—and my life's work.

The day was a warm and pleasant one in spring. It was a late Saturday afternoon, and I had taken a walk in order to enjoy the annual resurrection of green grass, colorful flowers, and blossoming trees. Actually, what prompted me to take the walk was the prospect of chapel service in the evening. The choice was to revel in the delicious air of spring or remain on campus and be forced to end a perfect day in a stuffy chapel. That was hardly a choice. The best way to skip chapel was to slip off campus a few hours before services. Besides, walking gave me a chance to sift through the maze of life, especially during those times when all paths seemed to run to dead ends.

A mountain of a problem rode upon my shoulders. Five years ago, at age thirteen, I had decided to be a minister. How paltry my knowledge of life then: the decision was that of a child in the wilderness. Certainly no one forced this choice upon me, but once made, it was not so easily undone. In the years since then, I had time for a lot of Soul-searching about the ministry as a life-long profession.

In looking back, it seemed impossible that four long years had passed since my arrival on campus, straight off the farm. As a child, I had a strong yearning for salvation, and that desire landed me here. I had completely taken to heart the Lutheran teaching of man's total depravity, and I was convinced that only a miracle or the ministry could redeem me of my sins. My hunger for salvation was just as strong today, but I now had a great many doubts about the ministry as the best way to attain it. With graduation coming in a few weeks, I faced this decision: to go on to junior college, which was also on the same campus, or quit.

The school was in Milwaukee, Wisconsin's largest city. Life there was a complete turnabout from the farm. In the city, row upon row of houses and buildings were jammed tight against each other, creating in me a burning need for the spaciousness of home. Soon after my arrival in Milwaukee, the bleak truth dawned on me: this city was to be my prison for the next six years. It was not a bad town; I just wanted freedom, like on the farm. But my parents would not hear of it, for which I am grateful today, because the preministerial school offered a better, all-around education for my future mission as the Mahanta, the Living ECK Master—the inner and outer spiritual guide for many—than did our country high school.

2

Here I was, a senior. With graduation but a few weeks off, the question heavy in my mind was this: Should I stand up to my family and bail out of religious study at graduation? Or would it be better to delay the fireworks and return to campus for two years of junior college? But could I stomach two more years?

So I took a walk to reflect upon this. Thus it was that on this pleasant day in spring I met the stranger. After walking fast for two hours, I was in strange territory somewhere in the suburbs. Hot and thirsty, I slowed down and began to look for water. On the left, set far back from the sidewalk, were the shade trees of a large municipal park. The trees offered a cool haven under their gently waving branches of new leaves. Beyond the stand of trees rose the naked steel ribs of a horticultural dome under construction. The structure loomed over the trees like a giant, delicate cup that someone had placed there upside down. There was an otherworldly aura of mystery about it, so I stopped on the sidewalk to observe it in silent wonder.

"A beauty, isn't she?" someone said behind me.

Turning, I saw a well-set man near forty, six feet in height, with chestnut hair and a broad face. His shirt and trousers were coarsely woven and forest green. He might have been mistaken for a construction worker or a gardener. Glancing around to see where he had come from so quickly, I saw no buildings, trees, or cars anywhere nearby.

"This botanical garden is in one of the largest municipal parks in the country," he said, his hand sweeping over the broad lawn. "Here are several hundred unusual rose bushes, and each year they plant thousands of annuals for seasonal floral displays." He told of the dwarf shrub, dahlia, and lilac collections. It seemed the stranger was every inch a gardener.

3

But then he pointed to the unfinished dome that soared above the trees in the background. Here, too, he was completely at home: The man was a walking encyclopedia on domed structures. His observations were sprinkled with words like vault, thrust, tension ring, tension members, spokes, and hubs—an amazing battery of construction lingo, to be sure.

The next switch was more up my alley. Artfully, he had turned the conversation from botany to architecture, and now, to religion. It was as if he had woven a garment from three unmatched pieces of fabric, and left no seams.

However, when the subject turned to religion, he was no longer the teacher giving a monologue, as he had on botany and architecture, but the listener. Soon he had me talking of my uncertainty about the future: to continue studying for the ministry, or what?

"How did you get into this anyway?" he asked.

How? Well, for several years now, I had convinced myself that the number-one reason I chose the ministry was because it offered a fail-safe passage to heaven. But the stranger's doubtful gaze made me review that position. So I made a quick run-through of the memory track and came up with this reason, a trite and petty one: it was actually because my cousin, for years the only other person in my grade school class, was going to be a minister. That meant he was going to leave home for a church school in the city. How unthinkable to break up our long friendship just because of that. So I decided to enroll there, too.

It was a jolt to realize that my years of homesickness were the result of such a frivolous decision. Concern for salvation may have been a consideration then, but only an unconscious one at best.

"Let me say this for the record," said the stranger. "You have a problem with salvation. On the one hand,

4

you believe that Lutherans are most likely to reach heaven; yet you doubt your own salvation."

An afternoon of discussing religion seldom has the power to cause a radical change in anyone's long-held beliefs. Still, what he said made me think. I had not solved the question of whether Lutherans were the most likely of all Christians to enter heaven. Did God smile more upon one group of Lutherans than another? For example, our country church was in the Missouri Synod. Our neighboring church to the north belonged to the rival Wisconsin Synod, while another in a town to the west was affiliated with the American Lutheran Church. Each congregation had a staunch faith in the articles of its denomination. And each believed that it alone enjoyed the closest allegiance with God.

I thought of God's love in terms of reaching out not so much to the individual, but to groups of people. At the top of the ladder of salvation stood the Lutherans (because I was one). But which of the Lutheran groups was foremost in the eyes of God? Probably the Missouri Synod (because I belonged to it).

The next step down the ladder, under the Lutherans, was a tricky one to choose. More than likely, one of the non-Lutheran Protestant churches would take second place, but surely not the Roman Catholics. They were the archenemies of all Lutherans, allies of Satan himself. The lowest possible rung was reserved for them. With the Catholics put in their place, this led to a further concern: What about salavation for heathens? What of people who, through no fault of their own, were born before the Reformation, before a Lutheran church was ever founded? And what of those people before Christ? All damned? Could God's love be so short-sighted as that of his children?

What was the mystery behind salvation?

5

I looked at the stranger, pleading in silence for a way to clear up my confusion. Unless someone gave a clue as to how God's love worked, I would drift forever before the winds of life. Nor would it matter a whole lot whether I wasted my time in a minister's gown or a farmer's overalls.

"Don't you suppose that God's love can transcend mankind's divisions of time, religion, or circumstance?" he asked. "All that you're certain of is that a great many people have lived on earth since the beginning, and a great number have died. The comings and goings of mankind are like the tides of the ocean. No matter what any religion says, one can see with his own eyes that Soul's entrances and departures go on as ever. Who among imperfect humanity can tell whether someone has advanced or fallen spiritually in his lifetime?

"The doctrines of religions are mainly beliefs spawned by the faulty imaginings of their creators. Each religion has something to offer to a chosen people of a given era, but that religion remains a splinter of the fullness of truth. If all man's teachings on salvation were added up, the sum of the parts would not equal truth. However, there is one teaching apart from these that outshines all others in the truth it contains, but this isn't the time to discuss it.

"Know this: God's love is sufficient unto all. Don't worry so much about your salvation. You're no better or worse than most people. Trust God to love you so much that you can learn to love yourself. One thing more, in a few years you will find salvation outside your church."

For some reason, I felt noticeably better. Was it his self-confidence that was catching? No, it seemed more that he carried the gift of joy and had passed it on to me. I felt light and good. My tiredness had slipped away during our conversation, and also my thirst. The sun

6

was setting in the west, and it suddenly occurred to me that darkness would fall before I got back to campus.

Only a little of all he said stayed in mind, but the gist of the message seemed to be this: Be confident of your salvation, which is in God's hands. Don't you know that His love is sufficient even for you? But my mind had dismissed his odd comment that I would find salvation outside the Lutheran church. If not for the prospect of falling darkness distracting me, I would have been shaken by the heresy of it.

As it was, I glanced at my watch. The stranger noticed, but said, "So what are your plans after graduation?"

His question brought me swiftly to earth. A decision about my future was still hanging. Nothing had been resolved.

Some people like to run and hide when faced by unhappy conditions. Rather than reconcile what has gone awry, they beat a retreat to an idyllic time in memory when life appeared sweeter. Whether or not they can actually return to such a past, they at least make the effort to do so in their imagination. Such dodging shows their unwillingness to tackle current situations of their own making. So when the stranger asked about my plans, I fled to the cave of a familiar past and said, "Go home to the farm."

"How long do you think you'd last there?" he asked.

How long? Why, the rest of my life. What else could I do? What would he do?

"If you asked me, and you haven't," he said, "I would finish school and forget the farm. Get your education. Later, you will have a better idea of what to do with the rest of your life."

Even though his solution made sense, I objected. "Another year will kill me."

"Will it? I could think of worse ways to spend the next four years. Think about it."

He turned to go. The feeling of spaciousness still remained, but my joy had mellowed into soft reflection, even sadness. Why be in low spirits about saying good-bye to a stranger met by chance one pleasant spring day? Why such a feeling that an old-time friend was taking leave, not to return again for years? But those were my feelings.

"You will forget today," he said, turning back. "But we will meet again." Then he left.

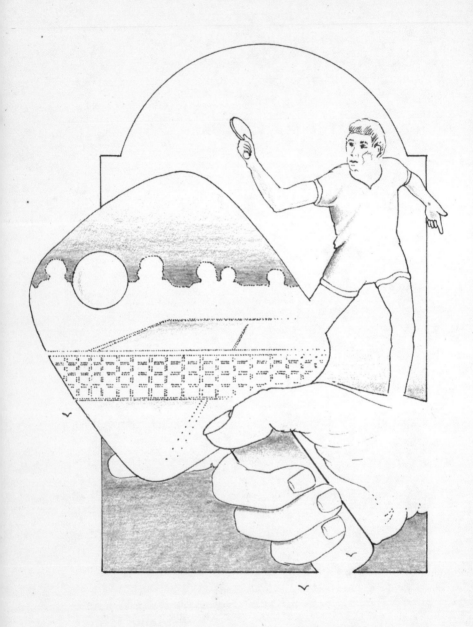

Who would think to look for a spiritual lesson in a Ping-Pong game?

2

Watch the Bouncing Ball

Ever so often the Mahanta, the Inner Master, will use our favorite pastime to teach a lesson of great spiritual value. This instruction may span years. If such coaching is spread over a long enough period of time, we may miss the wisdom behind it. This can create much confusion until we later see what the apparent setbacks were all about.

What follows is an example of how the Mahanta may teach the principles of ECK before a person comes into ECKANKAR.

The Mahanta wished to impress upon me the single-mindedness needed for God-Realization. To show that to me, three main experiences took place, and all of them occurred before I chanced upon the ECK teachings in 1967. They centered upon Ping-Pong, the game of table tennis.

The first experience took place during my sophomore year in college. A group of students asked me to organize a Ping-Pong tournament between two dormitories. Jim, whose skill ranged beyond that of most other players at school, lived in one dorm; I lived in the other. My playing ability, though not yet of Jim's caliber, had improved to where I was considered his main rival for the championship. The tournament began. Over the next few days, Jim and I played our way through the early rounds, defeating all opponents. At last, Jim and I were set to play each other in the final round for the championship.

Both dorms had a Ping-Pong table. The lighting in our dorm was good, but the room in which the table was placed was cramped. Conditions in the other dorm were just the opposite: bad lights, but much room around the table.

Jim, an easy-going person, liked to have a good time. When it came to Ping-Pong, however, he played without a shred of mercy for anyone. Therefore, it was a surprise when he said, "You pick the table."

What a nice guy, I thought.

After a quick mental survey of the strong and weak points of each game room, I said, "The lighting's better in my dorm; let's play there."

On the day of the big tournament, I was so nervous that the paddle in my hand felt like a hammer. Because of the room's odd shape, one wall was just inches from the table. The game began. As chivalrous as Jim had been in letting me chose the venue, he was just that ruthless in taking advantage of the closed-in table. Time and again, he hit the ball at a sharp angle—right into the wall—so it was impossible to return.

Jim hammered me with this merciless style of play. I was angry because of the shameless way he milked the crude playing conditions. My attention should have been upon winning. Disgust at his poor sportsmanship pulled my mind off the game until he won it hands down.

The memory of that defeat followed me for years. How many times did I replay that game in my mind—

always in a spacious, well-lighted place — and each time the victor? But there the daydream ended; nothing could alter the bitter memory in my mind. What was there to learn from this?

The second experience, another Ping-Pong tournament, came three years later. By then I was a senior at another college. A new time and place, it camouflaged the Mahanta's intent to develop in me a one-pointed mind so necessary to reach God-Realization. When the time came, nothing must be allowed to discourage me from that end. Someday, he knew, I would have every bit of tenacity needed to stick out the quest for God Awareness.

Players in this second tournament were again preministerial students, within a year or two of the seminary. Sweeping the early rounds of play, I was hardly worried about wrapping up first place: the field was weak. My opponent in the final play-off was Norm, a diminutive boy with a large birthmark on his right cheek. He was socially withdrawn because of it.

Unknown to me, the Inner Master was going to replay an old record: keep your emotions at bay and your mind in gear. Last time, my emotions had been upended because Jim took unfair advantage of a crowded Ping-Pong room. This time runaway emotions were my downfall again, due to pity for Norm's disfigurement. After a comfortable lead in the first game, I slacked off so he could catch up — to feed his self-respect. Norm's response was heartier than I expected, and he squeaked by to win the first round. We traded wins in the seven-game match, but in the last game I dallied too long. Near the end, after I had let him get close so he could have a better self-image, he made a few really brilliant plays and strutted off with the trophy. "Better luck next time," he said. His condescension made it indeed a bitter pill to swallow. Whenever I later thought about that loss, it brought me excruciating pain. But the game was over. Who would think to look for a spiritual lesson there?

The third occasion of the Mahanta's tutelage took place a year before I came upon the teachings of ECK. I was a new arrival at Misawa Air Base, Japan. One night, in the smoky game room on base, I played Ping-Pong with an airman and beat him repeatedly. He said his name was Leo. After several games he confided that he was sharpening his game for a regional Ping-Pong tournament near Tokyo. "You're good enough," he said. "Want me to get you in?"

Tokyo—an airman's dream. Leo's invitation was especially welcome because some airmen on base were harassing me at work and in the barracks. The tournament was a chance to leave the outpost at Misawa for a vacation. I jumped at his offer. The countless hours back at school spent at Ping-Pong instead of books were finally paying off. Even though a year had passed since I last played, and all the fine touches were gone, I was still good enough to beat Leo.

Our trip to Tokyo was not in first-class seating on a commercial airliner. Instead, Leo and I got a pass on a four-engined plane transporting airplane parts. The center of the cargo space was filled with a huge plane engine. Ropes tied to hooks in the walls secured it to prevent an accidental shift in flight. Around this mound of metal were lesser piles of gear earmarked for our destination. Our canvas folding seats lined both sides of the cargo space; this allowed a handful of us airmen to squeeze in. Rough air caused the tethered engine to strain at its moorings, leaving us to wonder whether a rope might snap and dump the massive engine in our laps.

14

Leo and I felt relief when the plane settled upon the runway. Military hosts escorted us to separate barracks, and next morning the tournament got under way. Since one player had cancelled at the last minute, that left an uneven number of contenders and somebody was without a partner. The remedy was to draw straws. The person who drew the short one got a free pass in the first round of play. While a sergeant read a list of game rules, I fretted about Leo. Where was he? Everyone else was there. The tournament was a military function; all participants were expected to attend.

The sergeant made the announcement: "Since there is now an odd number of players, we'll draw straws for the bye."

Some twenty-odd players grouped around him to pick from the hat. I drew a long straw: meaning I would face an opponent. Leo had still not arrived when it came his turn to draw, but the sergeant worked around his absence. "Since the other airman from Misawa isn't here yet, Klemp will draw for him."

With mixed feelings I looked at the short straw in my hand. Leo had the bye. It automatically moved him up to the next level of play without the bother of facing an opponent. The rest of us muttered about his disgusting luck.

The sergeant continued, "We might as well draw straws for the second round, too."

Twenty-some airmen and I all drew a long straw for ourselves. The sergeant pointed at me to do my duty for Leo. I drew, then not believing my eyes, I stared at another short straw in my hand. Our disgust was complete. At that moment, Leo waltzed into the gym. "Hi, guys! Sorry I'm late—overslept." He couldn't understand our dark scowls until the sergeant broke the good news of his two passes. Leo did have the grace to thank me for his good fortune, but it wasn't easy for me to accept.

While Leo got two byes, I drew Steve. He ended up tournament champ: unspeakably bad luck for me. But at day's end, even though I had lost our match, it proved to be the closest of all his following matches. And it was in that first game that my unchecked emotions again ran off like wild horses, as they had already twice in the past.

Due to my year of absence from competitive play, my offensive game was zero. My smash was rusty and weak from disuse. What did remain was a strong defense: the ability to return practically every hard smash that came across the net. Often it meant racing back from the table fifteen or twenty feet. With only my defense to draw upon, I still led as the game went to extra points.

Just as I was ready to serve the ball and wrap up the game, the door at the rear of the auditorium banged open. In marched an airman bearing a huge trophy in his arms. My eyes opened wide at that huge symbol of triumph; it broke my concentration. My drive to win melted like warm Jell-O, and my serve missed the table. Just that quickly, Steve took the last two points. He had game one and went on to sweep not just our second match, but the tournament.

Later the sergeant took me aside and asked, "What happened? You had the game. How could you blow the last three points?" What was there to say?

* * *

The Mahanta had hidden a valuable lesson for me in the three Ping-Pong tournaments. At the time it was unclear, but years later, after I was in ECK, they were a reminder to check my emotions while in pursuit of any

16

desired goal. Little goals are dry runs for the greatest one of all: aspiring for the God state.

The lesson: If you are determined to tackle a goal, put your whole heart into it. Don't ever let your attention slip. To do so is to lose the goal.

Years later, this proved to be a priceless lesson. When divine love brought me to God Consciousness, the greatest of all treasures, it appeared to slip right through my hands: there for a moment and gone. But the Mahanta's training years earlier in Ping-Pong stayed with me. It taught me never to give up on a precious dream; never to look aside. And always, to face the SUGMAD.

Through Ping-Pong, the Mahanta had taught me this primary attribute of all who master themselves and reach the God state: a single-pointed mind.

When Ray nearly hit the lady carrying the groceries, it was our second warning not to go to the airport.

3

Fate's Unseen Hand

O ur road through life is often forked and takes many turns. As a young man, I — like many young people — wondered what I would become someday: farmer, minister, or what? Then along came a mandatory tour of duty in the military, and I felt lucky to be accepted as an airman rather than a foot soldier, for the war in Vietnam was heating up. I later wondered whether that part of my life was a design of destiny or of my own free will. In other words, how much of one's course in life is personal choice and how much of it is controlled by the unseen hand of fate?

And while serving as an airman, what influence finally discouraged me from taking private flying lessons? A benign force working to shape my future, or my own decision based upon human judgment?

In 1965, with less than a year in service, things began to happen to me that I did not understand.

*   *   *

People enter this world at birth at widely different levels of consciousness. Contrary to the laudable ideal of the American Declaration of Independence, all

19

people are not created equal. Not in the United States nor anywhere else. A study of ancient or modern history gives ample proof of inequality the world over. At birth, Soul automatically becomes part of a pecking order, for such order exists in every department of life. Soul, in Its newly born infant's body, awakens to an environment well-ordered to supply an ongoing spiritual education.

Soul enters this world to accomplish a collection of tasks. Taken as a whole, these assignments make up Its destiny. To set the tone for Its mission, Soul may come into either a healthy body or a sickly one; into comfortable means or poverty; with great intellect or a simple mind; with the favored color of skin for that era or not; once a male, again a female.

Destiny, as a concept, is waning in popularity in Western society today. People want to run their own lives. They want to shape their own tomorrows.

Yet they do not know about the meticulous Law of Karma. The manner in which conditions are chosen to implement their birth remains a mystery to them. By and large, the Lord of Karma—not the individual—is responsible for selecting the family through which Soul enters the physical plane. Like a guardian who administers a trust on behalf of an infant, he arranges for Soul to join a family which offers the best prospect for spiritual unfoldment. In making that selection, he is under no obligation to consider the feelings or imagined rights of the person so involved. To him, placement is a simple matter: The Law of Karma, which governs such stationing, is the law. It must be obeyed.

The primal seed for each incarnation is under the umbrella of destiny, known to us also as past-life karma. On a practical level, genetic, cultural, and social elements combine to determine Soul's position in this world. For people on the lower end of the survival scale,

20

the Lord of Karma alone chooses the time and place of rebirth. By definition, the survival scale is a yardstick of one's "can do" instincts. But karmic placement does allow some people a voice in their place of birth. These are the individuals near the top of the scale, who are always creative in some way—usually cheerful, upbeat people. Because of gains made in past-life unfoldment, they have won a say in choosing their present incarnation.

Destiny can be thought of as the equipment, talents, or gifts which a person brings to this life. It remains for each to use them wisely.

Even though the idea of destiny, or fate, is taboo in many Western circles today, it is a fact of spiritual life. Perhaps objections arise because people are confused about what it really is. Destiny controls the conditions at birth. Much of what an individual does after that is an exercise of free will. Free will may overcome the conditions of destiny, but first one must awaken his creative talents, through which he can then reshape his spiritual and material life.

To sum up, fate governs the conditions at a person's birth; free will allows a choice as to how he will move within and beyond them.

* * *

Before coming into ECKANKAR, I was largely unaware of the inner and outer forces that influence each individual. Like most people, I considered my decisions my own, with perhaps a little help from God when things got rough. But then things began to happen which left me perplexed. Whenever I tried to carry out certain plans, something seemed to block them, often in a dramatic fashion. This bewildered me. At the time, it was frustrating, but now I realize that the Mahanta,

21

the Living ECK Master was beginning to guide me toward my destiny: my life's work as spiritual leader of ECKANKAR. Destiny was ruling out the occupation of farmer, minister, and now it seemed, even pilot.

While an airman at Indiana University, I took stock of my situation. The Air Force was to be my employer for three more years. After discharge, I wanted something to show for this four-year block of time given to my country. Since an airman's pay was a trifling amount, I looked for something other than a savings account to carry home after four years. There simply would not be much money to set aside upon which to build a future.

The future was then a closed book to me. Whatever I did, it had to be a sensible plan. Maybe a pastime that could later turn into a career, as flying had led to a career for my older brother, a commercial pilot. Why not be one, too?

One day I discussed my plans with Ray, friend and classmate. Would he care to take flying lessons with me at the nearby Monroe County airport? Ray was not wild about the plan. An easy-going Texan with a slow drawl, he held reservations about the safety of flying. For one thing, he was prone to having accidents. Although he made light of the fact, bad luck did seem to shadow him in those days. Why tempt disaster? was his question. But, swayed by my enthusiasm, he finally agreed to go with me to the airport. Surely, no harm would come of just gathering a little information.

It had not yet occurred to me that my purpose in this life was to be something other than a pilot. Actually, my future was already sketched out; I had only to fill in the blanks.

ECK, which is the Expression of God, spoke to me through the voice of direct experience, trying to guide me away from flying. But I had not yet been attuned to

Its voice. When It did speak, through several dramatic events in everyday life, all I noticed was a succession of delays, all of which I supposed were there to be overcome. Later, after several close calls, the realization finally dawned on me that perhaps my life was not wholly my own. The ECK Masters were preparing me to enter the Order of Vairagi Adepts, to be a Co-worker with God.

* * *

The first of three minor nuisances to the rhythm of events began the Saturday that Ray and I had picked to go to the airport, which was far out in the country. Since neither of us owned a car, we had a long, hard debate about what transportation to use for the trip. Ray was in favor of taking motorbikes, which were for rent in Bloomington, a college town. But I shied away from unfamiliar things. "What do we know about motorbikes?" I asked. "How about just a plain bike?"

"Motorbikes," replied Ray stiffly, "aren't that hard to learn. Remember, we're thinking about learning how to fly a plane." A most solid argument.

So we set off on foot for downtown to rent motorbikes, each of us hiding his uncertainty about beginning a career as a pilot. At the rental shop, we studied the motorbikes with misgivings. The owner, seeing our hesitation and reluctant to rent expensive equipment to novices, asked, "Did you ever ride one of these?"

Thinking back to a disastrous bicycle trip of some weeks earlier, we replied, "Sort of, but not exactly like this." After all, how much different was the basic design of a bicycle from that of a motorbike?

Ray and I applied the full scope of our analytical minds upon every possible hazard that might happen on motorbikes. Could they really be that different to ride from bicycles? Ray still had a sour taste from the two bikes we had rented some weeks past for a fishing trip. They were so hard to pedal, it felt like riding up a steep, unending hill, even on the flat stretches. Ray bristled whenever he thought of the miles he had pushed his worthless piece of transportation that day. Besides, we caught no fish.

Gravely, we signed the rental papers; then we pushed our motorbikes out of the shop, whose entrance faced an alley. The alley seemed a safe place to launch our journey to the airport. Ray gave me a snap course on the handles: throttle, clutch, and brakes. Apparently, he had had a little experience with motorbikes. "Now, do this," he said, putting his right foot on the starter pedal, giving it a few savage kicks. The engine coughed, sputtered, then caught—its meek putt-putts evoking only the mildest confidence in its roadworthiness.

With a cheery wave, as the Red Baron might have saluted a wingman, Ray gunned his bike and jerked down the alley toward the street. Cautiously mimicking his maneuvers with the foreign-looking levers and starter pedal, I followed. The motorbike was like a bicycle, except for the need to coordinate several kinds of unfamiliar levers. They occupied my full attention, giving no time to read such things as traffic signs. At least, not until emerging from the alley. Ray and his motorbike were a little dot far down the street. How would I catch him?

As I was about to follow him, my eye caught sight of a one-way sign. Ray was headed down a one-way street the wrong way. Evidently, he discovered his mistake at the same time; several speeding cars, racing side-by-side, were blaring their horns and bearing down on him. Hitting his brakes, he swerved left, then completed a U-turn on the sidewalk, narrowly missing the bank of angry drivers. This was our first warning to forget the airport.

Intimidated by street traffic, Ray continued to drive on the sidewalk in order to return in my direction. As I waited for him from the shelter of the alley, he wobbled toward me, flashed a subdued grin, then shot on by, still on the sidewalk.

Meanwhile, an elderly woman, returning home from a shopping trip to the grocery store, was slowly making her way toward us with a bag of groceries in arm. Ray, intent on reading his motorbike's gauges, was not aware of an impending collision. Suddenly, with the agility of a mountain goat, the woman sprang to safety behind a street lamp, dropping her grocery bag. Ray, still deciphering his instruments, had not seen her desperate lunge and, unruffled, continued off into the distance. In a flash, the little woman scooped up the fallen bag of groceries. Although she had first appeared so helpless and sweet, she was now shaking a fist and shouting epithets befitting a stevedore. Humbled by her display of wrath and seeing she was unhurt, I opened the throttle on my bike and shot into the street—in the event she had formed a vendetta against other motorbike riders.

This incident was our second warning not to go to the airport.

Several blocks away, I found Ray parked alongside the curb, the nose of his motorbike angled into the street. Hunched over his handlebars, he struck the pose of a traffic cop lying in wait for speeders. These two close calls, both within minutes of beginning our trip, had dampened my already cool enthusiasm. I was not in the mood for games.

"We're not ready for this!" I declared. "Let's take them back."

"Look," said Ray, "we're already better than when we started. All we need is a little practice. Come on, we'll be OK in the country."

Reluctantly, I trailed him down the street. Abruptly, he pulled off into a school yard, where he signaled me to a stop. Loose gravel covered the spacious playground in front of the school. The area seemed excellent for practice. Only the block of concrete steps leading from the school and jutting into the yard posed a problem, but the obstacle seemed large enough to see easily and steer around. By now, Ray was circling the yard, increasing his speed with each successive lap. I gunned my bike and gave chase. Round and round the yard we sped: like on a wild merry-go-round. Several times, the uneven ground, made more treacherous by the loose gravel, had thrown my bike into a slide on turns.

Then, swinging too wide around a turn, I saw it come: the big block of concrete steps. Pulling the turn as tightly as possible, I watched things happen in slow motion. My fingers were locked onto the handgrips. Like a miracle, the block of concrete flashed by harmlessly, a blur of grey. Unnerved by the close call, I eased off the throttle and put on the brakes. Then, from behind, came a terrible scraping noise. Peering over my shoulder, I saw another scene play in slow motion. Ray was in the process of riding his bike sideways, because it was on its side, sliding through the gravel and raising a cloud of dust.

Vaulting from my bike, I ran to him. He rose from the ground, brushed off his clothes, and practiced his Russian—the language which the Air Force had sent us here to Indiana University to learn. Other than a few scratches, both Ray and his metal steed were unscathed. This was the third incident that the ECK had sent to discourage us from going to the airport to

26

inquire about flying lessons. But I couldn't hear It speak.

"We'd better get on to the airport," said Ray. "I've had enough practice."

Leaving the city along back streets, we finally emerged into the glorious countryside. Traffic was sparse along the hilly rural roads. Our minibikes, not a threat to any speed records, were still fast enough for our inexperience. But out there, in the fresh air and wide open spaces, I began to feel the joy and freedom that comes with riding a motorcycle. Soon we were in top spirits. It was positively exhilarating to fly up and down the tree-lined country roads.

Then I began to play a game with Ray. While racing down one hill to the crest of another, I let him start a little ahead of me. Our bikes were evenly matched on the straightaway: Neither of us was able to outrun the other. However, while descending a steep hill and trailing Ray by several lengths, it occurred to me to duck down on my bike to cut wind resistance. Immediately I surged forward. As we drew abreast, I sat bolt upright, so he would not catch on to my secret.

"My win!" I shouted, then laughed at Ray's annoyance as momentum carried me past him.

Exuberance had made us reckless. The motorbikes were not merely glorified bicycles; they could travel much faster than bikes. But we felt safe out there in God's country.

Ray's bike had begun to lose power up one hill, and he fell behind. Then the hills disappeared, replaced by sharp curves. With an urge to race on alone, I wondered how fast my motorbike could take the curves. Waving to Ray, I opened the throttle and felt the excitement of taking corners at full speed. It never occurred to me that a patch of loose gravel might cause an accident, as had happened to Ray at the school yard.

Then came a tight curve, much sharper than it had first appeared. In desperation, I clung to the bike, watching it swing ever closer to the yawning ditch. As I left the road, something unusual happened. When the bike hit the shoulder, instead of skidding out of control and throwing me into the ditch, it jumped to the left and continued onto the road. Something had pushed me out of harm's way. Only after coming into ECK a few years later did I recognize this as the Mahanta's protection. All I could think of then was: *What a close shave!* With a more serious mien, I continued along the road to find a place in the shade to calm down and wait for Ray.

Five minutes later, Ray still had not come. I did not want to appear like a mother hen, but he should have already arrived—unless something had happened to him. Fidgeting on my bike, I made ready to start back to look for him when a car approached slowly from that direction. I flagged it down. Inside was a family out for a drive in the country.

"See anybody back up the road on a motorbike?" I asked.

"There were some people by the road a ways back," the driver volunteered. "Maybe he's with them."

No crowd had been outside when I drove the road a few minutes ago. For whatever reason they gathered, why would Ray stop to join them? Something was wrong. Kicking the starter pedal, I chugged back along the road, carefully scrutinizing the brush that lined the ditches around curves. A curve had almost done me in; perhaps Ray was not so lucky. But the vegetation alongside the road looked undisturbed.

Up ahead was the crowd the driver had mentioned. There seemed to be a picnic on the lawn, with a knot of people grouped around a family storyteller. Although reluctant to barge in on a private gathering, I thought that perhaps someone in the crowd might know of Ray's whereabouts.

As I coasted up to the driveway, the scene seemed to take on a surrealistic quality. Sometimes in the past, when coming upon a scene of injury, I had noticed that the atmosphere carried an otherworldly feeling. Objects would seem especially bright, coaxing me to notice their utmost clarity. First of all, the mailbox was out of place. Broken off, it lay on the ground. Near it was a motorbike, as if someone had thrown it down in a heap, instead of carefully standing it on its kickstand where it belonged. And there, surrounded by laughing people, sat Ray—telling stories and jokes. How had he managed to strike up such a camaraderie with strangers in so little time?

Then I saw the red gash on his forehead. Instantly all the pieces of this jumbled scene fell into place. Skid marks from his motorbike showed where he had left the road, narrowly missed a telephone pole, and then decked the mailbox. He was lucky to be alive. A motherly woman put a compress to his head, while Ray, with his droll sense of humor, continued to throw his audience one-liners. He had apparently escaped serious injury.

After composing himself, Ray lurched from the ground to inspect his rented bike. The collision had bent the right footrest under the starter pedal, preventing him from starting his bike. Miles from town, it meant pushing a heavy bike a long way. Besides, damage to the gearshift pedal had locked the bike into high gear, making it impossible to downshift into first and second gear in order to accelerate—had it even started.

Somehow the afternoon had slipped away. That evening, of all times, I had been assigned CQ (charge-of-quarters) duties at our detachment. Even though

29

students at Indiana University, we were housed in a small Air Force complex that contained dorms, classrooms, and an orderly room. Night and weekend CQ duties fell to airmen on a rotating basis. The CQ took charge of our detachment when the regular office staff went home at day's end. He and an assistant handled phone calls, carried messages, and were responsible for the grounds at night. Not to report for duty was a serious infraction.

Laboriously, we pushed our bikes to the crest of a hill. Time continued to march on, and I became very concerned about our slow pace. At this rate, I would be AWOL (absent without leave) from CQ duties.

Pressed by time, I now had an inspiration. Perhaps Ray could depress the clutch and coast downhill, thereby bypassing the need for first and second gear. When his bike hit road speed, he could pop the clutch. I hoped this would simultaneously start his bike and lick the acceleration problem. All Ray had to do then was open the throttle and keep it open. Momentum would carry him over the next hill, one of the last few steep ones before the road leveled out. We would be home free.

While we discussed these plans, Ray had been rubbing his right forearm, complaining of stiffness in the wrist. The countryside was devoid of homes, otherwise we might simply have phoned a classmate to bring Ray home by car. As it was, we were left to our own devices. And the clock kept ticking.

Ray coasted down the hill, and when he reached road speed, he let out the clutch. This engaged the gears, which turned the motor over and started it. The plan had worked to perfection: Ray was riding under power. Following closely on my bike, I noticed that his throttle was only partially open as he started up the grade of the next hill.

"Give her gas!" I shouted above the din of the two machines. He struggled with the hand throttle, but it did not respond. Perhaps it had also been damaged by the mailbox. With a sputter, his bike coughed and stopped just shy of the hilltop. While I checked the mechanical condition of his throttle, Ray again complained of a stiff wrist. He could not get a tight grip on the throttle.

"Look," I said, "I've got CQ. Can you get back alone?"

"If I'm not back by dark," he said, "send the APs for me." This was a joke, because our detachment was too small for air police — unless he meant the CQ, who would be me. The plan of starting and accelerating his bike had worked without a hitch the first time; no reason it shouldn't again.

"I'd like to rest a little first," he added. "Go on ahead. I'll see you later." Reluctantly, I mounted my bike and rode off.

Later that evening, Ray dropped by the orderly room to fill me in on the details of his return. His wrist had continued to hurt, and he ended up pushing his bike a lot farther than planned. To add to his woes, the proprietor of the rental shop had a shrieking fit when Ray showed him the handiwork of the mailbox upon the motorbike. A rip in the plastic seat cover, which we had not noticed earlier, was also disclosed. After soothing the irate owner, Ray left the shop and ran into some buddies returning to the detachment. Seeing his wrist, they urged him to have it checked at the campus clinic. But the nurse there pronounced it a simple sprain: nothing to fret over. All in all, Ray concluded, it had been a day to forget. The following day was not so good either: an X-ray showed his wrist was broken.

* * *

The injury naturally put Ray out of commission. It was a good reason to forget about becoming a pilot, which the Inner Master had been trying to warn him was not a good idea at that time.

The Mahanta had issued me the same warning, but he let me struggle on a while longer. Opposition continued to dog my plans to earn a private pilot's license. When the first sergeant at the detachment heard of my plans to fly, he called me into his office. Reminding me of the high cost of language training to the Air Force, he said, "What if you crash? What about our investment?" Angered by what I took to be an intrusion into my personal affairs, since the lessons were in off-duty hours, I sidestepped his objections by using a fictitious name on the schedule board at the airport. That way, if he called to check whether I was scheduled for flying lessons, the airport receptionist could not inadvertently give me away.

This arrangement allowed me to pursue the flying lessons, but they were spiced with a few heart-stopping experiences. In the brief eight-and-a-half hours of flying time before my solo, I narrowly missed several in-flight accidents—none of which were my fault. But that's another story. Eventually, while in Japan, I gave up flying when the obstacles became almost impossible.

* * *

The ECK had been guiding my life during all these experiences. Piloting aircraft was not to be my career. I was being trained to guide Souls. While I did all within my power to overcome the odd delays that mysteriously cropped up to stop my flying lessons, the Mahanta still gave his protection when danger threatened.

In time I would better understand the ways of Spirit. It speaks, but people are not trained to hear.

Often, the Voice of God is sent through the experience of everyday living. Few people have the consciousness to recognize It. Eventually, an individual unfolds to the point where he can both see and hear the Voice of God— as Light and Sound. He can then make great strides toward the spiritual liberation he has sought for so long.

The problems Ray and I had encountered in trying to get to the airport were really safeguards meant for our overall welfare. But we were so intent upon overcoming this opposition by the exercise of our free will that we missed the warning.

Until one learns to hear the Voice of God clearly, he is destined to wander forever in life—a child lost in the wilderness. When you put your life into the care of ECK, It will place you where your experiences in life will be the most rewarding. Then you will learn the difference between destiny and free will.

Imagine that you are climbing to the top of a broad green mountain.

4

A Short Spiritual Exercise to Try

This is a good place to add a simple spiritual exercise. It is for all who want to begin opening themselves to the Light and Sound of God.

The ECK (Holy Spirit) is the Light and Sound. God speaks to mankind—indeed, to all living creatures—through this Light and Sound. We could not live without the divine Light any more than we could without sunlight; or without the vibration of Sound, whether or not it is consciously heard or felt. The Sound, like the Light, is always present with us. To reach the highest spiritual unfoldment, we must become aware of both the Sound and Light.

This is a technique of imagination. To do this spiritual exercise, find a quiet room in your home where no one will disturb you for ten or fifteen minutes. Then shut your eyes and look at a place just above and between your eyebrows. That is the location of your Spiritual Eye.

Now imagine that you are climbing to the top of a broad green mountain. Follow the brown dirt path to a meadow of colorful flowers. Powder-white clouds near the summit of the mountain give a feeling of great joy, wonder, and freedom. This is the Mountain of God. When you reach the top, lie down upon the thick, soft carpet of grass. Feel the sunshine warm your face, arms, and body. Shut your eyes there, too, as you did when you began this contemplation exercise in your room. For the moment, expect complete darkness in your inner vision.

Now look gently for the Light of God to appear in your Spiritual Eye. It may appear in a number of ways. It may come as a soft field of light, similar to the fluffy white clouds near the mountaintop. Again, it may be a pinpoint of light: blue, white, yellow, purple, or even green or pink. While looking for the Light, softly sing HU (Hugh-h-h-h) over and over again. It is Soul's love song to God. Without staring, continue to watch for the Light within your Spiritual Eye. Listen also for the Sound.

The Sound of God is the vibration of Spirit moving the atoms of life. You may hear the sound of a flute, a rushing wind, the chirping of birds, a waterfall, bells, or the buzzing of bees. These are actual, not imaginary, sounds.

After ten or fifteen minutes, stop your spiritual exercise. It is unlikely that you will see or hear anything the first few times, but set aside time for the exercise daily. Do not overdo it. To spend hours at a time in contemplation is not at all desirable. This is an active world, and we must remain active to participate in it. The sole purpose of this exercise is to awaken you to the Light and Sound of God, making you a happier, more complete individual.

Return to the Mountain of God for a few minutes every day. That journey in contemplation is one of the surest ways to find divine love.

When Frank blew cigar smoke into my face, I had to confront my weakness of not wanting to face unpleasant circumstances.

5

Frank's Cigar

The incident with Frank's cigar took place about a year and a half before I had ever heard of Paul Twitchell and the spiritual teachings of ECK. Nonetheless, the Mahanta was already beginning to shore up certain areas in my spiritual life. For one thing, due to my religious development, I felt that God had a special love for the poor in spirit. My efforts at reaching this idealistic state of humility had produced a Charlie Brown, the boy in the cartoon strip whose personality is like mashed potatoes without butter or gravy.

The Mahanta recognized the slavery of spirit in my passivity. He knew I would soon be drawn to ECKANKAR. And like any seeker of truth, I had to find the strength to challenge the dark forces that would try to hold me from the Light and Sound of God. So he allowed a situation in my life to run to its extreme, forcing me to deal with my overdone meekness.

The Air Force security base at San Angelo, Texas, was just the place to catch the spirit of self-reliance. It was the last stop for my class of sixty airmen before we shipped out to permanent bases overseas. Basic training was long over, as were nine additional months of language school at Indiana University. By now, we were fed up with training and wanted to get on with life. But first, it was necessary to take several months of radio school here at San Angelo.

Soon after our flight of sixty airmen had arrived on base, it was broken down into eight squads. To my dismay, I was named one of eight squad leaders. Our duties were simple: to march our small classes of seven or eight airmen to the mess hall for breakfast. After chow, our squads combined into full flight formation for the march to class. Thankfully, someone else became flight leader. I was uneasy in any role that placed me above my fellow airmen.

It was here, in this environment, that the Mahanta chose to teach me a little about having a better opinion of myself. He did this indirectly, through Frank.

Frank, an airman in my squad, fancied himself a leader of men, long overdue for a leadership position. But, for the most part, he was a windy peacock—a petty troublemaker who felt more qualified to be a squad leader than me. That, however, was something neither he nor I could change. The order had come from the orderly room, where the first sergeant administered such details. Nobody went to him and said, "Hey, Sarge, how about making me a squad leader?" The position was so minor that the "First Shirt" would have pitched any such petitioner into the street. But Frank wanted my job, even though there was no way for him to get it. Therefore, my only recourse was to ignore him and his adolescent game of nit-picking whenever possible during duty and off-duty hours.

To keep my mind off Frank's barbs in the classroom, I buried myself in the study of radio technology. The instructor did not permit horseplay, but Frank fired his verbal jabs at me any time the instructor turned his back to write on the blackboard.

40

Reviewing this situation later, I knew that most people shy away from trouble. Many of us desire tranquility, which stems from an unconscious memory of paradise in an all-but-forgotten golden age. The memory itself is harmless, unless it makes us powerless to act in the face of an enemy who plans our destruction. This docile frame of mind must be overcome before anyone can hope to move forward on the path to God.

Isn't it uncanny how life picks the one opponent who can highlight our greatest weakness? Frank was it for me. No matter where I turned, Frank was there to badger me with his phony airs.

Thus, the ECK selects a battleground where each of us must undergo our baptism of fire. Every one of our failings is set against a human opponent. After the smoke of battle clears, we emerge as either the victor or the defeated: stronger or weaker. In this way are we cleansed in the crucible of ECK. This ECK is the Holy Spirit, which manages our unfoldment up and down the scale of God. We may think of the Mahanta as the personalized ECK. He is the Divine Essence manifested in a form that humanity may understand. Speaking in broad terms, the ECK and the Mahanta are one. In this broad sense also, Paul—the Mahanta, the Living ECK Master until his translation (death) in 1971—was guiding my spiritual life before I actually recognized him in 1967.

As the weeks of radio school dragged by, Frank's efforts in the classroom were average; mine, better. It was as if Frank couldn't zero in on his goals. His way of getting ahead was to step on others. He never considered that a little honest effort might be a better way of getting recognition. Instead, he kept the edge of his tongue razor sharp, using biting sarcasm on all who annoyed him.

41

For a long time, I had weathered his spiteful attempts to belittle me as squad leader. But it was today that we were to meet on a common battleground. He needed to learn to stay out of others' business, while my lesson was to learn to stand up to brazen, loud-mouthed people like him. The meeting ground was our classroom, on the day of the final radio exam. The Mahanta had stretched this lesson over several months, and not until this final class did Frank and I begin to settle our differences.

Our flight leader had marched us to the stockade where the final exam was to be held. We broke formation outside the fence-enclosed property that housed several classrooms. Barbed wire topped the chain-link fences in this top-security area. Filing into the class-room, we sat down at our desks, under the vigilant eye of our instructor.

"You have a few minutes to study," he said. "I'm going next door to get the tests. Squad leaders are in charge." Then he disappeared through a side door.

I sat off to the left side of the room. Frank and two of his buddies had seats directly in front of mine. They laughed and joked, but I used every precious minute to cram myself full of facts that might appear on the final.

"Look at Harold," said Frank. "He thinks a couple more minutes will make a difference."

There was generally an easy give-and-take attitude in our class of sixty airmen. As in any large group, small cliques formed among members of the class, but they got along with each other. Therefore, Frank's buddies were also mine. They did not take part in his harrassment now, even though he looked to them for approval whenever he made fun of me. But I kept my nose in my notes. Over the weeks, I had learned how to tune Frank out, just like a noisy radio station. If nothing else, the radio class taught me to recognize an important radio broadcast, but also to block out any interference. And that's what I did now with Frank.

His words made no impact on me. Then he put his hand on my desk and shook it. I glared but said nothing. Made more bold by my apparent passivity, he shook it again.

"Hands off," I warned.

"Oh! Listen to Harold," he said in mock surprise. "He's getting rough." Then he looked to his companions for backing, but all he got in response were thin smiles. An unwritten code in service is that everyone must handle his own trouble. If an aggressor violates the bounds of fair play, then one may expect help from others; otherwise, it is his own battle. This was mine.

My weakness was that I did not like to face unpleasant circumstances. There is a parasitic group of people that can spot such victims in an instant. Such parasites include freeloaders who drop in for dinner without the courtesy of a phone call. Other parasites ask for a handout after they have squandered their own money. Still others weasel themselves into positions of trust in their company, then leak information to outsiders who would destroy the company, and do it in such a way as to make the wronged feel apologetic. These are God's brassy creatures. But eventually they overstep their bounds. Not knowing where to stop in their greed, they drive their quarry to the wall and a battle ensues. The aggressor is astonished at the fury of his victim, and so must beat a hasty retreat if he is to come out of the fracas in one piece. That's exactly where Frank and I were now.

Any minute the instructor was due back in the room. Frank kept goading me, certain of my timidity. He was sure I would just sit there and simmer while he amused himself at my expense.

He lit up a cigar. Big clouds of smoke billowed into the room. Then he turned and blew a cloud at me. When would the instructor get back? Another cloud of smoke wafted at me like a blanket of filth.

Frank was at the height of cheer. He knew there was no way I could respond to his provocations. If the instructor came in the door, I would appear to be the instigator; he, the victim. But Frank went a step too far, and I saw red. This, remember, was before I got into ECKANKAR and began to learn the virtue of controlling anger.

My notebook was open on the desk in front of me. Very slowly, Frank turned in his chair. In his hand the cigar was tilted up so the ashes wouldn't fall off. Then he flicked the hot ashes onto my papers. He turned back to his friends and rocked with convulsions of laughter. Lean smiles continued to line their faces as they wondered what I would do.

I looked at the ashes on my notebook. Very carefully I lifted the notebook from the desk to be rid of the ashes. Just as Frank turned in his chair to see my response to his mischief, I threw the cigar ashes in his face. He jerked his head back, sputtered, then coughed. His eyes began to swim with tears from the irritation of the ashes. Frank's face turned red, about the same color as mine had been.

"Oh, Harold's getting brave now," he said. "Think you're tough? Let's see just how tough."

My voice was even, quiet—but my chin had begun to tremble. It upset me that I couldn't control it. "I'm right here, Frank. Anytime."

Suddenly, I had a feeling of great strength. It was the inherited strength of my father when he got into his wild rages. During those times, he had the strength of several men. And I was now in such a rage. There was

44

no fear. All movement appeared slowed to one-fifth of normal. My adrenaline was so pumped up that everything else seemed slow by comparison. I saw how the fight would go. There would be no wild swinging on my part. Whatever Frank could do was of no concern. I was certain that nothing he would do could hurt me for the instant it would take to grab him by the collar and belt, then loft him high up against the classroom wall. And Frank could see this look in my eye.

"Come on, Frank."

"Look! His chin's shaking. He's so scared he can't control himself."

"Look again, Frank."

He laughed uneasily and turned to face forward in his chair. The fight was over before it began.

A minute later, the instructor came into the classroom, which was now unnaturally still. He looked around, sensing something had happened during his absence, but no one gave any indication of trouble.

No matter what Frank may have learned from this encounter, I learned that fear is not something out there: It is a monster inside us. Until it is conquered in its lair, we will always be failures to some extent in whatever we set out to do in life. The Mahanta, through the indirect method of Frank's aggressiveness, had brought this lesson home to me.

It is good that Frank and I had this confrontation. When our orders came in, we were shipped to the same overseas base. There we served in the same unit and worked together every day. Finally, when a few airmen were chosen to transfer to Yokota Air Base near Tokyo, the two of us were among the few who actually went— out of a field of several hundred who had been on the original list.

In this way, the ECK taught me that nothing happens by coincidence in the life of one who seeks truth.

45

The Mahanta knew that Frank and I would be working together in the future. He also knew that it was our respective weaknesses that made us enemies. If either of us was to advance spiritually, we would have to face that weakness inside ourselves.

And we did. We became good friends the rest of the time we were in service. The credit goes to the Mahanta, and to Frank's cigar.

A green frog, embracing a bright yellow floor lamp,
was starting to give me a religious awakening!

6

The Downside of Drinking

Military service is a great homogenizer. It takes young people and exposes them to sundry sides of life. They learn quickly what they might otherwise not learn except at the cost of many years. Some of these experiences are of spiritual help, while many others are not. But taken as a whole, they all contribute to the enrichment of Soul.

Drinking alcohol is not beneficial spiritually. People frequently use alcohol as a pacifier when they are unable to contend with loneliness, discontent, or failure; its use is common in the military. It beclouds the mind and can drop a person to the level of a beast in no time at all. Anyone who is serious about building a higher spiritual life for himself will not dull his awareness by using alcoholic beverages. Drinking alcohol is the act of hiding from something. A God-seeker must learn to hide from neither himself nor his problems.

My own background with alcohol as a German descendant was largely restricted to beer, which had always seemed to be a pretty harmless substance. But being accustomed to it later paved the way to an overdose of bourbon. This happened in the Air Force, about

49

three months before I came into ECKANKAR. Since then, I've come to observe that alcohol is a drug which hinders one from using his full God-given abilities.

Even worse, it may cause one to have psychic experiences which can bring fear or spiritual harm to the abuser.

I arrived in Japan early in 1966, following a year and a half of training at three stateside locations. My first assignment was at Misawa Air Base near a small town on the northeastern tip of Honshu, the chief island of Japan. About six months later, just as the tops of the mountains to the west were beginning to whiten with snow, I was one of a few lucky airmen to receive orders to go south to Tokyo. In Misawa, I had seen airmen at their best and, more often, their worst behavior. The base was classified as remote, meaning that it was far removed from the social interaction that airmen were used to at home in the States.

The usual tour of duty at Misawa was two years, and young airmen found themselves separated from family and friends for perhaps the longest time ever. To compensate for homesickness, a natural result of this separation, many airmen divided their time into three not necessarily equal parts: work, bars, and sleep. After work they cleaned up and slipped into civilian clothes to make for town and bar row, which was conveniently located outside the military gates. Once in town, they engaged in drunken revels that lasted the better part of two years, until a new set of orders returned them to the States. Drinking turned many of these young men into brutes. Had their families been able to drop in on their sons downtown, they would have returned home with some shocking memories.

Trouble seemed to divide itself along the line of how much one drank. In general, the heaviest drinkers were often the worst troublemakers.

Two forces pulled at me in regard to drink. On the one hand, my family was of German descent, where beer was considered the milk of heaven. Pulling the other way were the years I'd spent on a church campus. The Lutheran church, even though of German origin, realized that its future pastors must develop moderation in regard to drink. My observations of young airmen who were destroying their lives with drunkenness cooled me toward excesses in drinking. Why not be fully conscious of living? Usually I preferred soft drinks over beer, hardly ever stooping to hard liquor. At heart, I was essentially a man of the cloth.

With winter nipping the mountains in the west, a rumor began to circulate in the operations building about a task force to be sent to Yokota Air Base near Tokyo. It would be a permanent, not temporary, assignment. Scores of airmen begged for this plum mission, because Tokyo offered everything to an airman; Misawa, close to nothing.

The hand of ECK was certainly at work. As a new arrival at Misawa, on base only six months, I was at the foot of the priority list. Despite all logic, I outlasted a lengthy system of selection and was one of the lucky airmen to end up at Yokota.

My situation at Yokota was both new and interesting. Our newly formed group, although small, was composed not only of airmen, but also of Army and Navy men. And in an unusual turn of events, not only did we work together, we were also housed in the same barracks. In the two-man room directly across the hall from me were two Army men, Willie and Casey, and we soon forged a close friendship. Our conditions at work were pleasant, and the days and weeks flew by until it was suddenly the end of summer.

About this time I began to hear of Paul Twitchell and Soul Travel for the first time. There was an article on him in *Fate* magazine. Then Brad Steiger included a piece about him in one of his books, where he portrayed Paul as a teacher of Soul Travel. This slant immediately caught my fancy. The desire to learn how to transcend the human body and explore the regions of God gave my life a new direction. In the Air Force my attendance at church service had dropped off to nearly nothing. Perhaps years of morning and evening worship at school had filled me to the limit. Whatever the reason, it was a relief not to attend church, even though I had a few pangs of guilt about it. Unconsciously, however, I began to place my hopes on ECKANKAR to fulfill my spiritual needs.

The church was going out as a power in my life. My social life, courtesy of the airmen's club, where beer, entertainment, and bingo were available, was acceptable, if not fulfilling. I was adrift on the sea of life—but always reaching to find new meaning in existence. Therefore, Paul Twitchell and Soul Travel offered something new and exciting in the way of spiritual adventure. But it would take a sharp rap alongside my head before I could accept the fact that my ship was sailing before the winds of life without a rudder. To continue a voyage like that could only end in disaster.

It was during my Air Force years that I got enough distance between myself and the frenetic daily ritual of orthodox worship to question what religion could really offer me. I came to realize that no matter what church an individual belonged to, his expression of faith was unlike that of any other person.

There are all kinds of Lutherans, all kinds of Catholics, and all kinds of Hindus. Each group has a range of conservatives and liberals. Overall, the people in a group are more alike than not. Lutheranism for me was certainly not a religion of modern-day miracles or spiritual exploits, even though such events were common during New Testament times. From my perspective, the Holy Spirit had retired from active duty, disdaining the displays of pomp and majesty It had enjoyed centuries ago. Today, all a Lutheran was required to do was be responsible to God and family, and believe that Jesus was his savior. Sallies of faith were neither required nor wanted. The Lutheran church was not established for people who wanted to experience the Light and Sound, as had the apostles and early Christians at Pentecost. It offered a simple faith. All useful knowledge about God had already been revealed to our church fathers ages ago.

The spiritual life I sought, and was soon to find in ECKANKAR, was a universal teaching. Guilt kept people in line in the Lutheran church, but was the tax of fear too stiff to pay? What about a spiritual path that exalted a positive virtue for moral action instead of fear? What about self-responsibility as a substitute for fear to give one a reason to seek a better life?

Casey and Willie were hardly my intellectual companions at Yokota. For that I relied upon Hubie, an amiable person with an extraordinary mind. We often talked about spiritual matters, but it was at a level so apart from daily living that I often wondered how an atheist could possibly call himself one and not sooner or later commit suicide. Hubie was not an atheist. His personal universe, however, was so filled with the possibilities of what a person could accomplish by his own means, that there was little room or need for God. In his universe, I felt like a guest at the wrong party. Somewhere between the two philosophical positions—the blind faith of the Lutherans vs Hubie's belief that he was sufficient to structure his universe without the help of divine assistance—was a place I might feel at home. Looking back, perhaps Hubie's outlook on spirituality was a higher one than what I then perceived the Lutheran faith to be.

Willie was something else. Where Hubie was cerebral, Willie was a practical GI who was hell-bent on having a good time; but at work he was quick and efficient. The summer of 1967, Willie put in a request to go to Vietnam on temporary duty to be the bus driver for the squadron. That earned a ribbon showing he had served in the war zone. At the time, there was little threat to the safety of the drivers.

My supervisor had offered me the same opportunity. Maybe the experience would have been good, but I became upset when military personnel stationed in Japan, a veritable paradise, begged for a stopover in Vietnam to win a tiny ribbon. That ribbon implied they had encountered the same risks as soldiers in the infantry and air cavalry units, who were dropped into the jungle by helicopter and had to fight their way out again. It especially galled me because my youngest brother and a cousin his age were such frontline soldiers in Vietnam. They faced mortar attacks, snipers, and jungle fevers.

For a while, I was an unpopular figure in my unit. I finally realized the unfairness of making my associates feel guilty because they did not have loved ones there in danger.

The first night Willie was gone, the barracks felt empty. Willie was full of life, full of mischief. Things were always buzzing with him around. About eight in the evening, I knocked on Casey's door to see how he was getting on with his roommate gone. Casey was reclining on his bed, a quart of bourbon in hand, listening to music on his stereo. Casey was the quiet counterpart to Willie. Both liked alcohol, but Casey was a quiet drinker. Wearing a perpetual sheepish grin on his face, it was hard to tell whether he was drunk or sober. He was a pleasant fellow from Chicago with disarming grey eyes: a man who steered clear of trouble. At work he carried his weight.

Our shift had just gone on a three-day break. For me, this usually meant catching up on reading in the library, listening to my stereo, or sometimes catching a bus to nearby Johnson Air Base to take in a movie. For Casey, the break meant three days of drinking. It was a way to forget home.

"How about a drink?" he asked. Usually I said no, which made me an oddity among my friends, but tonight we were both feeling the blues because of Willie's absence. Beer was generally my limit, since I deemed it less harmful than hard liquor. If I drank at all, it was for company. Without being aware of it, my strong taste for beer, which came from my German heritage, was lessening during the last months in service. Even though I had not yet heard of ECKANKAR, the Mahanta had already begun taking me into the inner worlds to teach me from the Shariyat-Ki-Sugmad, the ECK scriptures. The changes outwardly were hardly noticeable at first, but a night like tonight would make me very aware of how easily alcohol could reduce one to the state of an animal.

When I returned with my mug from next door, Casey poured it half full. "Want to go to the midnight movie?" he asked.

Movies were shown at 12:30 in the morning because the base ran shifts around the clock. Airmen who were relieved from duty at midnight had just enough time to catch a late meal at the chow hall, then rush to the base theater.

Thus our evening was planned. There was a four-hour wait until showtime, so we shot the breeze, trading stories about our experiences as civilians and GIs. When the bourbon reached the bottom of my mug, Casey leaned over genially with the bottle to automatically replenish it. Neither of us had paid much attention to the quantity of bourbon we had downed until the bottle was empty. Casey studied it in wonder. By now the time was 9:30.

"It's three hours till the movie," he said. "Let me borrow your bike. I'll get us another bottle from the airmen's club."

My bicycle, a treasured possession, was my transportation to work. Long ago, I had made it a policy not to lend it to anyone: other people were careless and damaged it. This exclusion meant everyone. An indication that my judgment was affected by my part of the quart of whiskey was revealed when I unhesitatingly handed Casey the key to the bike lock. From my room, which overlooked the bicycle rack, I could watch Casey grope in the dark for the chain, mount my bike, then wave cheerily as he wobbled off into the night.

A half hour later he returned, weaving more than when he had left, a brown paper bag clutched to his chest. I was waiting for him by the bike rack, relieved to see that he had returned my bicycle without a scratch. By eleven o'clock, most of the second bottle was gone. Talking was now more difficult: words began to slur and come out funny, causing us to laugh, but our eyelids were drooping at the same time. It never occurred to us that we might each have consumed a near-lethal dose of alcohol. The bourbon was just there in our hands, to sip while we waited for the movie.

"Maybe we should get a pizza," he suggested.

By 11:30, the pizza man knocked on the door, and Casey collected himself to count out the right amount of money. Before the midnight hour, our pizza was history—as were Casey and I. Casey toppled over on his bunk, an angelic smile pickled on his lips.

"Still going to the show?" I asked. In response, his eyes glazed over and he passed out.

Feeling suddenly very weary, I gathered up my shaving kit, went to the washroom, and cleaned up for the night. There was no point in going to the movie alone. On my way back to the room, I checked to see whether Casey was OK. He was still curled up on his bunk, right where he'd collapsed. To make him more comfortable, I shoved his feet onto the bed and began to cover him with a blanket. This roused him. Looking at me with suspicion, and obviously without recognition, he reached back to his hip pocket to secure his wallet.

"Your money's all there," I said, to reassure him.

He froze in position, his hand gripping the wallet in his pocket; then his eyes frosted over and he pitched forward onto the bed, out for the night. "You're in bad shape, Casey," I rebuked him in parting. I made my way gingerly to my room. The floor rolled like the deck of a ship at sea.

"Whoa!" I said out loud. "Captain says there's a storm tonight."

And brew it did. I reached my bunk safely, and carefully balanced on the edge of the mattress, I removed my clothes. Stacking them as neatly as possible on a chair, I also fell into bed. Everything went black.

This night was going to both frighten me and teach a lesson. I knew that alcohol dulled the senses, but not that great quantities of it were a poison that could actually drive a person from his body, propelling him into a bizarre dimension. It would also show me that my understanding, built upon the cut-and-dried dogma of the Lutheran church, was not enough to explain away the phenomena of invisible worlds. Until now, I never took seriously the possibility of existence beyond what could be seen or touched in the physical world. In a word, I was a pragmatist.

Before dawn, I would be reminded of inner forces that round out mankind's existence.

Three years had passed since my vision in college, in which an Old Testament fortress appeared upon the clouds. A voice spoke, and the gates of the fortress slowly opened to reveal more. The vision rocked my ideas about Divine Spirit being a dead force of the past. That incident is told in *The Wind of Change,* in the chapter "A Question of Salvation." The shock of that experience had shaken me awake spiritually, but the wound had healed. All that remained was a fragmented knowledge that things might exist outside the neatly bound package of Lutheran doctrine.

About 2:30 in the morning I awoke with a start. The bed felt slimy. Making a supreme effort, I reached over to turn on a desk lamp. At first it seemed my eyes were playing tricks: the sheets, the once-white wall, the rug, and the wooden floor were all colored red. Groggily I reached for my glasses and was disgusted to find I had thrown up my pizza while asleep.

The room was a pig sty. Luckily, each barracks was equipped with a washer and a dryer, so I bundled up the soiled bedsheets, careful not to get any of the half-digested tomato sauce from the pizza on my T-shirt. The airman who lived next to the laundry room had his door open and was engaged in a late-night bull session with a buddy.

As I strode by with the load of dirty linens, one of them exclaimed, "Good God!"

But I paid them no mind and stuffed the clothes into the washer, set the dials, then returned to my room. Perhaps I could clean up the mess before anyone saw it.

Once in my room, I noticed that my T-shirt felt cold and sticky. Pulling it off, I saw the reason for the airman's exclamation a few minutes earlier. My shirt, still clean in front, was smeared a horrible catsup red in back.

Well, never mind, I thought. By morning this mess will be gone.

It was hard to manuever. Only a few hours had passed since I succumbed to the bourbon; nevertheless, I dug up a mop, put soap in a bucket of hot water, and began the laborious job of scrubbing up. Midway through cleanup I became sick again but was able to reach the latrine and spare myself a further cleanup. In the meantime the clothes were washed, so I tossed them into the dryer and returned to my bunk to rest while they dried.

Then a strange thing happened. The moment my eyes shut, an apparition appeared. A green frog, straight from a cartoon and as tall as my knee, was embracing a bright yellow floor lamp, whose round base had a message in red ink. As I squinted at the letters, the frog thoughtfully tilted the lamp to make reading easier; but as he did so, the ink began to run, obscuring the message.

Startled, I snapped my eyes open. This sort of thing was never covered in religion class. Although the frog was no theologian, he was starting to give me a religious awakening.

The frog's appearance frightened me badly. My mind began to race, the way it used to when I was a child. It often sped up so fast that I was afraid it might spin away and leave me behind. Those childhood nightmares were especially frightening because there was no way to tell anyone about them. My mother could only hug me until I calmed down and fell asleep.

Now, on my bunk, it worried me that my mind might wind up and run away even while I was awake. Perhaps it would slow down if I busied myself with something. The room still smelled sour from the vomit, so I decided to clean the place a second time. Even though desperately tired, I was too frightened to sleep. So I refilled the bucket with soap and water, again scouring the floor, metal posts of the bed, and wall. When the sheets were dry, I made the bed. Time had slipped away; dawn was creeping up the eastern horizon.

It's daylight, I thought. Maybe sleep will come now.

I lay back on my bunk. However, no sooner had I shut my eyes than another strange scene appeared in front of me. This time I was standing alongside a long mountain trail. Coming up it stretched a long line of people, each moving at the rate their age allowed. Oddly, these people looked like grey wisps of fog. It was like looking at them through a thin white curtain; indeed, from another dimension. As for me, I had no body at all. In its place was a soft ball of hazy light. Although the climbers came within touching distance, none of them noticed me. It was as if I, not they, were the ghost. Old and young, men and women, all came steadily up the trail, heading purposefully for a destination which seemed to be the top of the mountain.

These inner sights revolted me. Feeling that I was losing touch with reality, I reopened my eyes to the comforting familiarity of my room.

By now I was sweating with fear. It was the weekend; airmen were sleeping in. I needed to talk with someone to regain a sense of how things should be. Casey was still passed out next door. Nauseous again, I retreated to the latrine a second time. Fatigue was overpowering; it was impossible to stay awake. Anyway, the sun was now well above the horizon and maybe this would allow me to catch a nap.

The moment my eyes shut a third time, however, there was a scene that I later determined rose from a past life. It was a room with two windows at the far end. Standing between them was a man clothed in European dress from what appeared to be about the 1800s. Instinctively, I sensed that this man was none other than myself in a previous lifetime, even though I still had little knowledge about reincarnation at the time. To even consider reading about past lives was to provoke the ire of the Lutheran God who ruled my universe. The well-set man in the quaint clothing wore a flat-topped hat upon his head and sported a grey swallowtail overcoat, unbuttoned because he was indoors. The man's frank expression was not in the least bit threatening. He observed me calmly, even as I studied him with frank curiosity.

This experience left me too agitated to sleep. Considering all the liquor, and the few hours of recuperative sleep, I was in remarkably good shape: not at all stiff from a hangover.

What was the effect of this experience upon me? In a very frightening way the alcohol had poisoned me, allowing me to penetrate the invisible worlds, which I hardly knew existed since I had not yet heard about the teachings of ECK. Although I did not see much while in these invisible realms, it was enough to impress upon me there were still unknown things on earth that awaited discovery. The night diminished my taste for liquor, and beer began to further lose its hold on me. At the same time I recognized that earth is truly a place for Soul to get experience. A world of unknowns, earth is a place where one may create for himself a kingdom of spiritual wealth or a pit of slavery.

One thing seemed certain: the abuse of alcohol can drive a person to conditions he may neither understand nor be strong enough to face. For me, this night was an upsetting visit to the lower Astral Plane, but it was also

61

another step in preparing me to appreciate ECKANKAR and the high teachings of ECK when I finally came across them.

When mother finished speaking, I said, "I'm not taking communion; I'm leaving the church."

7

Good-bye Church, Good-bye Farm

Ever since I found the ECKANKAR teachings in 1967, the ECK slowly but surely leveled the ruts of habit that had me off on a roundabout way spiritually. Two years later, I had pretty well drained the resources to be found in the Lutheran church. All that remained was to get up the nerve to break the potent social and emotional strings tied to me. The ECK, however, was there to help.

The ECK, or the Holy Spirit, is the clean, life-giving force from the Mountain of God that sweeps into the valleys of mankind to purify all spiritual stagnation. This is the heavenly wind of God. It began to root up my old life of discontent and direct me toward spiritual liberation. This ultimately meant a freedom from myself. In my case, it was necessary first to overcome the social pressures of church and family before the way was clear to move onward to a new life in ECK.

In 1968, my four-year stint in the Air Force was over. Far too much of that time seemed to have been spent inside windowless offices on air bases, and I was now ready for the rejuvenating sunshine of home.

65

Following my discharge at Fort Meade, Maryland, I made a beeline to the farm.

But freedom was a long time in coming. It turned out that I had only traded one harness for another.

A tour of duty in the Air Force had made big changes in this one-time student of religion. One of those concerned religion itself. Four years earlier, when I left home for the Air Force, it was under the shadow of having turned my back upon the ministry. "How can you just quit?" my parents and relatives demanded to know. "Look at the wasted time and money."

Now I was a different person. After my return, they began to hear about Edgar Cayce, Paul Brunton, and the Rosicrucians. But the final straw was Paul Twitchell. To them, he, ECKANKAR, and Soul Travel were creations of the devil. The ECK teachings seemed to pose an outstanding threat to their beliefs. Yet they did what they could to tone down their hostility toward ECKANKAR because of my help on the farm. They also condoned my reading of what they considered heathen ideologies because of my regular church attendance. The family was driven by the great social leveler: "What will people say?" My steady appearance at church would forestall any embarrassing questions by neighbors.

My religious beliefs had expanded while in the Air Force, but there was yet another change. The Air Force had also shown me how to handle real-life problems better. Its conditioning of mind and body gave me confidence: I could match the other airmen in the performance of duties. And under certain conditions, my gifts of intuition put me in a class by myself.

But at home, Dad regarded me in the same light of inexperience as when I had left for my tour of duty. To him I was still a child. Accordingly, he gave orders and expected me to obey them: no questions asked. That's how it had been once; why change things now? His mind; my muscle. Any suggestions I made to ease the work nearly always met with a storm of rage. The Air Force had shown me easy ways to approach a task, and it was natural to try such economies of motion on the farm. Dad was adamant: the work would be done *his* way.

In the Air Force I had thus gained a new outlook on religion and on work. However, the farm squelched any chance of further growth along either of these lines. In a nutshell, the family's view on religion was: "Jesus is Lord—that's all you need to know." Dad's view of farming was equally cut-and-dried: "Dammit, I told you what to do. Now do it!"

The expected freedom and development was simply not to be found on the farm. In the meantime, I spent hours in study every night in a small upstairs room, plugging away at a course on business management. Someday, whether on the farm or not, I knew it would come in handy.

Following my discharge from the Air Force, it took only a few days to settle into a comfortable routine, helping to pick corn and work up the land. How good to be home! The Second ECK Worldwide Seminar would be in Las Vegas a few weeks later, but I passed it up. Once home I seemed caught in a web and put off travel plans until it was too late. This was no great disappointment, for Paul was still largely an unknown factor in my life. While it would have been nice to meet him, the thought of such a meeting left me uneasy. I sensed that any physical encounter with the Mahanta would burst the seams of my world and leave me completely unfit for the cramped spiritual, intellectual, and emotional life offered me on the farm.

The weeks and months of 1969 slipped by. My desire for spiritual freedom deepened as I read the ECK books. Yet while my inner range of vision was growing, external forces were backing me into a corner. It was like a long tunnel that got smaller the further one walked into it. Sooner or later, the two extremes of my inner and outer life must collide. There was no way around it. The wild tugging of these forces was like a match between two wrestlers, each trying his best to win.

When it came, the conflict was between my parents, relatives, and church on the one hand, and ECKANKAR and me on the other. During the first year home on the farm, I had gone to church every Sunday and religious holiday. But the longer I studied ECK, the more experiences I had with Soul Travel and the Light and Sound of ECK. The greater my firsthand knowledge of heaven, the less need for the old religion.

In October 1969, I asked Dad for time off to attend the Third Worldwide Seminar in Los Angeles. By now I was more sure of the love and power of ECK. What Paul Twitchell had said about Soul Travel and other aspects of ECK were true: I knew that from personal experience. Yet the family's opposition to Paul made it a most delicate thing to ask for the weekend off.

"What do you want there?" asked Dad suspiciously.

Hiding my true reasons, I explained, "I want to find out, once and for all, if Paul Twitchell is really what he says he is." That soothed him.

The Sunday of the seminar, when neighbors at church asked my whereabouts, my parents assured them I was not sick, but at a seminar in Los Angeles. Then my parents artfully turned the conversation to safer matters.

In fact, I had gone to Los Angeles to get the Second Initiation from Paul. On the plane home, I made a firm decision never to take communion again. It seemed the best way to express my feelings about the church and begin the steps to leave it. But the ECK said no; the time was not yet right. There were still a few karmic bills to repay on the farm. Until they were off the books, this chapter of experience must go on.

This is how the ECK said no: The day after my return from the ECKANKAR seminar, I broke my right arm while cranking the tractor. A freak accident, it forced me to remain on the farm. Plans to quit the church and then look for work in a nearby town vaporized with that one backfire of an engine. Now there would be more communion services after all.

And so, engaged in learning the ECK philosophy of life, I had to follow out the consequences of this injury. For the next two months I helped do chores with one arm in a sling. But milking cows was out. It simply did not work to hang a milker on a cow with my arm in a cast. But I did climb up the slippery ladder of the silo, a pick and fork tied to my waist, to throw down silage. The silage was frozen, so I swung the pick with my left hand to chip it loose, then threw it down the chute with the fork tucked awkwardly under my good arm. Normally a half-hour job, it now took two hours to complete. Our hay was baled, so I threw bales down from the haymow and broke them up for the cattle the next morning during barn cleaning.

No matter how laborious my broken arm made the simplest winter task, I did whatever possible to carry my weight on the farm, to make the most of a bad situation.

The doctor finally cut the cast off. It was a shock to see how my right hand had shrunk: it looked like the claw of a big rat. The broken arm brought an alarming realization of the hairline between life and death.

Anything at all might snuff out this fragile existence with a puff.

This injury magnified my desire for ECK. I had felt only fear and uncertainty about the afterlife while a Christian; but since becoming an ECKist, I knew that if a person died, he did not linger in a dark grave until the Judgment. The body was only a house for Soul. And I was Soul. When my body died, I would be instantly free to roam the universes of God. There was no need to wait in a grave for a day of judgment before life could proceed again. ECK is Life—here and always.

This is not to say that only ECKists are privileged to go on with life immediately after death—people of other religions do too. But an ECKist knows it, while others may not. For many, death is a black hole of delayed existence—a concept which offers absolutely no consolation, only fear and dismay.

The condition of my shriveled arm pointed to weeks of recuperation on the farm. Dad had aged greatly during the two years I was in Japan, so he could use help with chores until spring. By then, another of my brothers would be home from service, maybe to help run the farm.

One Sunday, near the end of winter when my arm was strong again, our pastor held a communion service in church. I sat up in the choir loft with the young people, as far in back as humanly possible. The balcony gave a bird's-eye view of those I had known all my life. There were the shiny bald pates of Dad and Emil, the bouncing heads of Elmer and Dorothy's kids, and all the other people I'd never see like this again. In that instant I knew this was the last time I would ever take communion. It was a last reflective look at friends and neighbors as one of them. To leave the church meant to sever the one cord we had in common. After the next communion service, I would be an outcast: a frightening but sad thought.

Communion service was usually scheduled every two months. I lived in dread of the next one, because that was my deadline to quit the Lutheran church. Now came the self-doubt. Wasn't there always time to change plans? Until I spoke of mine, no one would be the wiser. A weak but comforting fancy.

Inwardly I knew there could be no turning back. Life had me on the ropes. Like an adolescent who is neither child nor adult, it was a sobering decision to leave the security of church for the uncertainties of the new spiritual path of ECKANKAR. Yet I knew Paul was the Mahanta, the true agent of God. The Sound and Light had demonstrated that to me again and again.

My announcement to quit the church came one night at supper. Mother had the food on the table when Dad, two of my brothers now home from service, and I came in from chores. Dad gave a blessing and we all said ours in turn, as was our custom since childhood. Then Mother mentioned her intention to call the pastor to announce us for communion on Sunday: a standard practice. The moment had come. It was time to tell my parents I would not go to communion again.

They should have seen it coming, and maybe they did. For one thing, last fall Dad saw me refuse a bottle of beer while picking corn for Arnold, an elderly neighbor. This was practically unheard of in a German community. At noon, when we had gone into the house for dinner, Arnold handed me an ice-cold beer from the refrigerator. When I said no thanks, he was surprised and a little hurt—a slap in the face. Was I feeling OK? He rummaged in his well-stocked refrigerator, produced a soft drink, and offered it instead. I expressed my thanks, but his puzzled look said, That stuff's for kids.

Another forewarning to my parents and relatives of my changing values took place after the Third Worldwide Seminar, where I got the Second Initiation. Paul asked all Second Initiates and above to fast on Fridays. He suggested three kinds of fasts and left it up to each person to choose the one best for him. First was the mental fast. With it, one would center his thoughts upon holy and good things all day. Second, the partial fast. This could either be one meal that day or else fruit and fruit juices. Third, the water fast. Light fasting, he said, helped to work off karma and quicken spiritual unfoldment. I chose the water fast, which meant only water for twenty-four hours. It is understandable how this might have upset my family, because of the empty chair at mealtime.

Mother's plan to announce us for communion was a formality, because it was unthinkable that anyone might not go. The meal had just begun. My brothers and I had been piling food on our plates to eat in the living room in front of the TV. When mother finished speaking, I said, "I'm not taking communion; I'm leaving the church."

Her fork dropped on the plate with a clatter. "Oh, Harold," she wailed. "Not that, too?"

She felt it was enough of a sin to even read the "heathen" works of ECKANKAR, but to brazenly leave the church? Well, that was like asking God for a ticket on an express to hell.

My brothers picked up their plates and vanished into the living room, out of the line of fire. Trying to be as sympathetic as possible, I weathered the tears and protests of my parents. But when they blamed that devil Paul Twitchell for everything, I carted my plate off into the living room to join my brothers. Maligning Paul for my decision was blind, unfair anger.

72

Thus began a siege. Over the next weeks, my parents missed few chances to warn me about the fate of an unredeemed sinner after death. During this time of pain, I continued with the Spiritual Exercises of ECK, because there was no other upliftment for me. The Sound and Light of God were always there, but it still marked a very lonely time in my life.

Quitting the church was best for me; staying in it was right for them. Soon thereafter, the once-idyllic life I had sought on the farm drew to an end. The ECK was closing an old chapter in my life and turning the page for a new one to begin.

The light coming into my room was the Light of ECK,
the Holy Spirit.

8

A Dog's Life

How was my inner life going at this time?
Soul Travel, as always, was my passion. No matter what, I was determined to become a seasoned traveler in the Far Country, the heavens of God. And as with everything else I had ever liked to do, I put my heart into it fully. All this time, Paul had been coming to me in the Soul body, helping me out of the physical shell. Something I found interesting was that no two Soul Travel experiences were ever exactly alike. Never. There are so many possible ways to Soul Travel, and such an endless variety of things to do, that I found it at once an education of the highest sort and interesting as well.

A Soul Travel experience may have had any of a hundred different reasons for happening, but it always showed me something about myself or my condition. It was never boring.

ECK initiates sometimes write to me today of an experience that frightens them. They want to be assured they'll have only pleasant times on the inner planes. It would be wonderful if it could be that way in every department of their lives, but that's not how life is. Life teaches us to face our fears. How can that be done unless a person confronts the very thing that has kept him from the higher realizations of God?

When I was going through the separation from the church, the one solace besides my cat friends on the farm was the Spiritual Exercises of ECK. The exercises were only a means to an end: through them I met Paul Twitchell on the inner planes. If I had no friend in the neighborhood because of my beliefs, there was always Paul, who was the Inner Master. But all the experiences he gave me in Soul Travel were not necessarily happy ones. They did, however, give me strength to endure what could not be avoided. One such was the following experience.

Chores were done; the family was in the house reading the paper or watching TV. About 9:30 I said good night and went upstairs to my room. The floorboards of the old house creaked with every step, an advantage: an early warning system if Mother decided to come up for something she needed downstairs. My room was cold: It was not unusual for me to see my breath. There was an old space heater in the room, but I didn't use it except for very cold nights because of the fire hazard. In my flannel pajamas and bathrobe, I sat on the rug beside the bed, wrapped in a blanket like an Indian at his campfire.

My spiritual exercises were generally done in two parts. The first part was sitting in contemplation beside the bed for up to an hour. It's easy for a single person to do that, but harder when one is married. Whether having some experience at bedside with the Sound and Light or not, I continued the spiritual exercise in bed. The usual length of time that I lay in an alert state, not letting myself drop off to sleep, was anywhere from an hour to several hours. No matter what it took, I was willing to make the commitment to travel in the other worlds.

Generally I sang my personal word. Every Second Initiate receives a spiritual word for contemplation that fits his state of consciousness at that time. If my word didn't seem to work, or when I had a nudge to use another word for variety, I frequently used *HU* or *SUGMAD;* otherwise *Paul, Rebazar,* or any other ECK Master's name that came to mind. But regardless of the word, I always entered a state of alert expectation. Each session had the potential for bringing a Soul Travel experience. This I knew. Hopeful expectation must become the heart of one's spiritual exercise.

On this particular night, I finished the exercise on the floor, avoided the floorboards that squeaked, and climbed into bed. *HU* was the word I chanted that night with my eyes shut. Suddenly, as if a skylight had been opened into the ceiling, a vast dark sky reached above me. I continued to chant *HU,* my thoughts upon the goodness and love of Paul, who was then the Godman.

The blackness of the sky was pierced by a thin beam of white light. The light came down through space, right into the room. Careful to keep myself calm, I watched the light with a sense of curiosity. It was the Light of ECK, the Holy Spirit. Even if there would be no more to the experience, It was purifying me spiritually. And so I rested in bed, content to observe the white beam of light that shone steadily into my room on this cold winter night.

The light then changed: It began to spread out in a circle. The sky became lighter in the center, but the edges remained pitch-black. The white beam became a diffused light, with a soft blue light around its edges.

Next followed the sensation of rapid movement. My physical eyes were shut, but my Spiritual Eye was open: I could see everything plainly. In spite of the feeling of moving upward, the lightened sky remained just where it was. Now a golden light surrounded the blue, so that only the very outermost edges of the sky remained black. When the golden light came into view, I felt myself being lowered from a high place to somewhere below. Then the light was snuffed out and all was dark.

A great stillness was all around me. Wondering what to expect, I opened my eyes. Instead of being in the bedroom, I found myself in a brightly lit pet shop. In the Soul form, I was two things at once: a point of view on the ceiling, and also a physical being. But the being I was, was not a human.

To my surprise, I found I was in the body of a puppy. The store was closed for some reason. Nobody was around. I was locked in a wire cage about three feet long and high, and two feet wide. Besides my ability to see, there was something stronger here: a feeling of great loneliness. It seemed that I had been in this cage forever, forgotten by everyone. I would have given anything to see someone enter the shop, open my cage, and take me away. Besides having the ability to see and hear, I also had the awareness of time. It stood still. For ages, it seemed, I lay in the small wire cage, my heart almost breaking from loneliness, and no one there to release me.

Time on the Astral Plane, where I was during this Soul Travel experience, runs on a separate band from that on earth. A few minutes on earth can be days in the other worlds.

This was the dual consciousness. Usually it's thought of as a split between the physical and inner awareness, but this was me: a human who knew he was locked inside the body of a puppy. I knew the keen sense of lonesomeness an animal might feel in a pet shop or a dog pound. It was about the most unloved, abandoned feeling I had ever known.

About this time I began to call on Paul to set me free. For all I knew, I was trapped in this puppy's body for good. What my parents might discover the next morning was beyond conjecture: maybe a son with the consciousness of a little dog? And the person who bought the puppy? Perhaps he'd be the owner of an unusually bright dog who read a lot. Despite my predicament, my mind couldn't help but play with the possibilities.

Then I realized how miserable a person might be if he were transported to another century by a time machine. Or just as bad, if he were an ECK initiate in a strong Lutheran community.

For hours I sat in that cage, a helpless pup. I could understand the desperation a prisoner might feel in his cell. After what seemed ages, there came a high sound of humming. It was the Sound of ECK. My sight went dark and things in inner space began to move quickly. Then came the sensation of brakes being applied, like a courteous bus driver who stops gradually, a consideration to standing passengers. When I opened my eyes, I saw my bedroom ceiling. Suffice it to say I was overjoyed at my return to familiar surroundings.

For those who consider Soul Travel the product of an overactive imagination, I can only say that it is more real than anything one could imagine. Soul Travel is an aid to gain spiritual experience toward God-Realization. Many do not understand this: Soul Travel cannot take one all the way to God-Realization. It is simply a ladder set on the ground of the Physical Plane that reaches up to the Soul Plane. That's all.

People who know the letter of the ECK writings, but not the spirit of them, will say that "Paul said" Soul

Travel is how one reaches God Consciousness. Strictly speaking, this is impossible. Soul Travel is a way for Soul to move through the worlds of time and space, but the worlds beyond the Soul Plane are not of time and space. The problem we face in the spiritual works is having to speak to people in terms of motion and duration, because that's all they know. So we use words and expressions that hint at life above the Soul Plane but can never come close to describing it. The true spiritual worlds must be experienced, for they are regions of seeing, knowing, and being.

Yet Soul Travel is the highest method of spiritual travel known to mankind. It is in the keeping of the ECK Masters, who are the only ones able to give anyone this experience. It is broader in scope than Astral or mind travel. Each of those methods is limited to the plane of its origin. But with Soul Travel, a seeker can move at will throughout the lower planes—the Astral, Causal, Mental, and Etheric planes. Incidentally, these lower worlds include the Christian heaven on the Mental Plane.

Now what did this Soul Travel experience signify for me? First, it was an experience in the other worlds, where far stranger things are possible than one finding himself viewing the world from the body of a puppy. Second, this experience had another dimension: it gave me a broader perspective of my current problem of leaving the church.

I was like a helpless puppy in a pet shop. All the doors were locked by beings so much bigger than me. If they put me in a cage and locked the door, that was my cell. The Soul Travel experience made me confront the terrible loneliness this ostracism would cost me. The length of time that the experience lasted, seemingly for days, was the Mahanta's way of saying, You must stay here until the conditions are right for you to leave the church. What made that so hard to endure was not having a time schedule. That's why a child in kindergarten is so anxious for his parents to be on time after school, because every minute the child is there after the other children have gone seems like forever. The child does not have an adult's sense of time. If his parent shows up five minutes late, that can feel like an hour or a day.

Nevertheless, I was relieved to be in a human body again. But having been cooped away in a puppy made me grateful, and more patient, in my conflict with the church. All I cared about was whether Paul, the Mahanta, was with me. If he was, I could be placed anywhere and still find a measure of happiness.

How little I suspected that this experience was also a look at the near future.

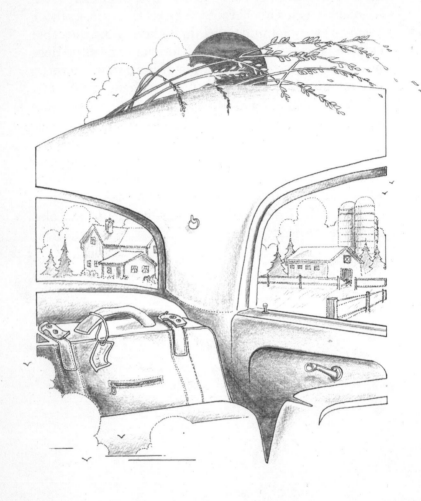

As we drove away, I felt a deep sadness. Why did life demand such painful choices?

9

The Squeeze Is On

The night I announced to my parents my plan to quit the church was the beginning of a tug-of-war: their will against mine.

It is remarkable how strong the fear of God is drummed into people. My parents were of the belief that my decision to leave the church was an automatic sentence to hell. That's what they were taught to believe. When, for instance, I once tried to explain to Dad that Luther's translation of the Bible was just one of many, and not even the earliest at that, he insisted, "It's still the best." It was remarkable how he could know that, since he seldom, if ever, read any Bible. But he was speaking on general principle, which needn't encumber itself with stuffy facts.

The first hurdle to cross after announcing my intention to leave the church would come on Sunday morning. Would I have the spunk to carry out my resolve and stay home when the family went to church?

Sunday morning, while the family dressed for church, I stayed in the barn to sweep the aisles. When their car left the driveway, I watched them go with an empty, consuming feeling in my stomach. At noon, when they returned from church, I was upstairs in my room. At mealtime, the tension around the table hummed like a high-speed motor. Eyes were red from crying. Filling my plate after Dad said the blessing, I retreated into the living room to take refuge in the sanctuary of a TV program.

One afternoon, Mother told me that she and Dad were going to our neighbors' that evening for a visit. This was unusual because it was no one's birthday. "What for?" I asked.

"The minister wants to talk to you. He's coming tonight." Just what I needed.

Our guest was the new minister, the vicar who had made a midlife career change from being an insurance salesman. Our old minister was about to retire. On cue, Dad and Mother said good night and left for the neighbors'. The vicar and I studied each other—he from Dad's rocking chair; I, from mine. The object of his visit was to convince me to drop my foolish ideas about ECKANKAR, whatever that was. Since he asked, I told him about Soul Travel. Our perspectives about the Bible came from disjoint ends. When I told him of the levels of heaven as reported by Saint Paul, who knew a man who had been caught up to the third heaven, the vicar brushed that information aside as of no consequence. It didn't matter how many heavens there were; the most important thing was to get to heaven. Details could be worked out later.

The vicar was a likeable man, but we were like two swordsmen—both fighting for my life. After we had parried arguments for several hours, the clock in the living room began to chime midnight. Through the window shone the headlights of a car. My parents had stretched their visit as long as possible and were now coming home.

The debate with the vicar on the merits of ECKANKAR vs the Lutheran church was about what one might expect between a vicar and an ex-preministerial student: a gutsy crossfire of arguments that did not persuade the other to change his convictions. But I had held my ground.

* * *

Now it became imperative to find a job and leave the farm. The older members of my family resorted to treating me with cold silence. Dad, however, agreed to let me take the car to town once or twice a week, but despite my search, nobody had a job opening.

When I asked Paul in contemplation what to do, he said, "There is a position for you at a publishing house." But I was too inexperienced to think of going to the phone book to check on a listing for publishers. So I groped around for a few more weeks, going to the wrong places, being interviewed by people who had no need of me. At one large company, the personnel director had me fill out an application. She reviewed it, made a phone call, and soon I was seated in the office of an executive who seemed to have a lot of time to spare. We talked for an hour, but if that was an interview, which I did not suspect at the time, I failed it. He finally led me to the door with regrets: "We'll keep you in mind."

To someone else that may have been a discouraging setback, but my faith in Paul as the Mahanta was such that I had every assurance that the right position was already waiting for me. If he said there was a job for me in publishing, then there was.

After each unsuccessful day of searching, I would return home and report the results. It was pitiful the way Dad's hopes rose at the bad news. For some reason, he had set his mind on me taking over the farm, even though both my brothers had more of a background in farming. On the other hand, it was precisely because of their years of working with him that they wanted no part of the farm.

Farm work was slow in winter, except for hauling in wood to fuel our furnace and kitchen stove. So on this particular day, I asked to borrow the car for another run into town. That was the day I found the publishing firm.

At the time I didn't know the difference between a publisher and a printer, so I began to drop in at printing plants to look for work. Many of the printers were still using old-fashioned hot metal for monotype and linotype. Somebody had to carry the heavy trays of type, and since I was strong on muscle and lean on experience, the most menial tasks seemed to be my lot. Eventually I landed in the personnel office of a large company that was both publisher and printer. The woman at the desk had me complete a form, then she placed a call. The production manager himself came to ask a lot of questions. As he spoke, I began to see the scope of the company's work. When I volunteered to carry trays of type, he said, "Let me call somebody. He may have a different job opening." First it sounded as if he were going to send me to another business firm, but moments later a round, gentle little man entered the room. He introduced himself as Milt, assistant supervisor of the proofroom.

"Do you know anything about proofreading?" he asked.

"I could always spell," I said, "but I've been away from books for a while."

The more he talked about proofreading, the more excited I became about it. "Come upstairs to the proofroom," said Milt. "While you're here I'd like to introduce you to the supervisor." The supervisor was George, a distinguished man who smoked a pipe. How fitting for a literary man, I thought.

"Say, Milt," said George, "give him the spelling test—and don't help him."

Later, I learned that Milt was a soft touch. But then, all the proofreaders were fine individuals. The spelling test was comprised of all the words people misspelled most often. When I finished the test, Milt scanned the paper, blinked, and whispered, "You spelled 'proof reader' wrong—it's one word." Obediently, I put the eraser to good use and made the two words into one, and Milt handed the quiz to George. George looked at the test over his bifocals and exclaimed, "Yes, very good. Very good, indeed. You didn't help him, Milt, did you?" Milt squirmed; George knew Milt.

Arrangements were made to have me start work the following Monday. At home, Mother and Dad had mixed feelings about my new job. "They're going to pay me to read," I said, hardly believing my good luck. Even though my parents did not sanction the direction my religious interests had taken, I *was* their son. They were happy the job fitted my talents and interests.

Before Monday, I drove into town again to look for a place to stay near the publishing house. Within walking distance, on a street lined with old houses, I found a sign in the window advertising a room for rent. The landlady showed me what was actually two rooms: a front room and the bedroom. The bedroom felt cold. A throw rug was on the right side of the bed, but the rest of the floor was bare. A large, scratched dresser was an arm's length from the bed, and beyond that, a portable closet. And a chair. All had seen better days. It was a depressing place, but it would serve until I could buy a car and move to a better part of town.

Sunday evening on the farm, I packed the few things I would wear at work. Church service had been an awkward time that morning, as usual, because I stayed home. Tonight, no one said, "When are you coming back to church?" They could see that I was slipping from their grasp. My brother, who already had a job in town, was waiting in the car to drop me off at my new place.

As we took off down the driveway, I felt a deep sadness at seeing all the bright things that might have been on the farm be left behind. This was the beginning of a new life, but the new hope it offered certainly was not accompanied by good cheer.

Why did life demand such painful choices?

Checking doubtful words in the dictionary took a lot of time, but it taught me to avoid assumptions.

10

A Proofreader's Bright, New Future

Spring had officially begun a few weeks before I started my new job as a proofreader, but in the Midwest, the calendar date is taken with a grain of salt. It was a raw, damp morning as I left my lodgings and began the long walk to the publishing company.

A thin blanket of dirty snow covered the postage-stamp-sized front lawn. The streets were aflow with cars taking their owners to work. Car windows were steamed up and drivers rubbed briskly at their windshields with the backs of gloved hands. I envied the drivers for their cars.

It had been a night of restless sleep: The room had a bad feeling about it. The landlady informed me that all her roomers had been around for years, yet there was a definite chill in the place. One might expect some warmth where people had chosen to live so long, but surprisingly, there was none. Her house was a haven for recluses who only wanted a bunk. Even though I did my spiritual exercises at bedtime, it was like doing them in the catacombs outside the gates of Rome: a hollowed-out shell of emotional decay.

The route to work took me over a long bridge. A chill penetrated my bones because the rush of cars caused the damp morning air to lash at me on the narrow sidewalk beside the roadway.

Warm air met me as I opened the door to my new workplace. In the proofroom, the supervisor directed me to a two-person desk near the front, out of the way until he got the day's work organized. I felt quite alone and out of place, wondering if I would be able to carry my weight proofreading, with no previous experience. Before the bell had rung to start the workday, a few employees came up to give me the inside track on how the place was run. It has been my experience not to jump at the first offer of friendship when coming to a new place of employment. The gossips are among the first in line with greetings. They pry loose whatever information possible in order to broadcast the inside scoop on new arrivals to other employees.

Training was considered a long-term project in the proofroom. A new employee was hired carefully. Once aboard, it was expected that he would be there a long time; therefore, his training was thorough. No one seemed in a rush to get me proofing that first week. Instead, the supervisor said, "Do you think you can learn the Greek alphabet? We publish a few fraternity and sorority newsletters, and you'll have to know a *phi* from a *psi*."

My lucky day, I thought. Thank you, Paul.

Paul Twitchell was always on my mind, because he was then the Mahanta, the Living ECK Master. My life since coming into ECK had been one of much upheaval, but I could see that the changes were beneficial: cutting away the fat so the spiritual life could thrive. With every painful change that came into my life, there always seemed a bridge to something better. Here I was to be a proofreader, highly uncertain of my ability to succeed, but the need to know the Greek alphabet fed right into my past skills. Greek was one of several languages I had studied over the years. Much of my knowledge of Greek had faded from disuse, but a little polishing should bring it right back.

At my dual proofreader's desk sat Karen, who was the number-one proofreader in the house. She was also the trainer for new employees. At the end of the day, I said to her, "I know the Greek alphabet. Ready to test me?"

Actually, they weren't ready to administer the test until Friday, because that's how long they hoped it would take me to master the unfamiliar Greek symbols: A trainee upset the work flow. They hoped I'd be quiet and keep out of the way. And when she finally gave the test, I passed easily. So she handed me the company's proofreading manual. "Tomorrow you can start learning the proofreader's marks," she said. "They're in here."

I took the manual home that night and studied the marks. The next morning, she gave me manuscripts to practice on. It took a bit to recall the mark for a certain use, but with practice I got better at it. What did slow me down was the long absence from reading and other mental pursuits. Spelling had always been my strong point, but now I had no confidence in what words were right or wrong. This meant having to check doubtful words in the dictionary, which took a lot of time, but the discipline formed good work habits. It taught me to avoid assumptions. When researching a question, it was worth the trouble to consult an authoritative source for the right answer. Because of my diligence in checking words and other details, by the time I left the company a year later, the supervisor told Karen that I had developed into the third- or fourth-best proof-reader. All those better than me had been on the job for more than five years. His acknowledgment of my proficiency was quite a compliment.

But the year in the proofroom was also going to prove the most tumultuous of my life. George, the supervisor, had laid out a plan for my future at the company. Because of my education and evident interest in publishing, he said, management would do whatever it could to help me into the white-collar ranks. I would be groomed for supervisor. But future events would ruin any chance of such potential.

The ECK wanted me to get certain experiences there, then move on to another place for others. My future was not to be in publishing. The ECK Masters were grooming me for a position far greater than proofroom supervisor.

The ECKANKAR Midwest Seminar was to be held in Chicago at the end of the month, April 23–26. I couldn't wait: another chance to see Paul. It was also the fulcrum on which the rest of my life would turn. If I had known then what I found out later by hard knocks, I might have let this seminar go by too, as I had the Second Worldwide Seminar.

Some proofreaders were a little put out that I got a weekend off the first month at work. What was this Midwest Seminar? When pressed, I finally said, "It's sponsored by ECKANKAR."

"ECKANKAR?"

"The Ancient Science of Soul Travel."

When word of that got around, my chances for a future as a supervisor wilted before my eyes. But more was to come.

The rose was the Master's gift given through the young woman.

11

The Midwest Seminar

The days before the Midwest Seminar in Chicago passed like molasses. It was quite nervy for a new employee to ask for time off less than a month after being hired, but that was a condition I had insisted on. The ECK seminar was scheduled for April 23 – 26, 1970—Thursday through Sunday. So on Wednesday night I took a cab to the bus station. It was the same station used for my vacation shuttles between home and Milwaukee years ago as a freshman in high school.

A few months ago, Paul had written me a note asking if I would be an ECK representative for Wisconsin. His request petrified me. Number one, I was terribly shy. Did this mean I would have to give talks to people with inquiries about ECK? This was really a test of my convictions. Soul Travel was the only thing about ECKANKAR that interested me. It was a personal study. Number two, being Paul's rep would put me into a more direct conflict with the family: that problem could only get worse if I tried to use the farm as a base for spreading the ECK message. It was bad enough when the mailman drove up with letters from the head-quarters in Las Vegas marked in red ink, "The Ancient

Science of Soul Travel." This man had brought our mail ever since I could remember. Each Soul Travel envelope met with raised eyebrows when I went out to the mailbox to retrieve it from the mailman's hand.

Fortunately, I had the good sense to consider my circumstances. Paul's request, I decided, did not mean, Drop everything now, take up a trumpet, and give the good news of ECK to the whole world—at any cost. Paul was the Mahanta, the Living ECK Master. He knew that one could not just take from the ECK forever without giving something in return. One could try, but his unfoldment would stop. Above all, ECKANKAR is a path of common sense. The Mahanta never expects someone to be erratic, nor to carry out any instruction without considering what effect that action might have upon others.

So I did nothing for the time being. Wisconsin reps were few: there was a couple in Milwaukee, another person ninety miles to the southwest of home, and me. It was a thin network from which to begin spreading the message of ECK in Wisconsin.

Paul's attempts to spread the message of ECK must have been difficult beyond belief. We four Wisconsin reps never accomplished much. We were like four blades of grass growing in a handful of dirt on a rocky mountainside. Too much rain, we'd wash away; too much wind, we'd blow away; too much sun, we'd burn away. We were ordinary people whose love for the Mahanta was thrusting us into the limelight. The thought of it terrified me. Yet guilt, which was instilled in me by religion, was steadily losing its hold; and I was willing to risk bumping into Paul at the seminar in the off chance he might ask, "Well, how are you doing in Wisconsin?" My hopeful response would be, "I have plans."

The bus ride was uneventful. The station was near the hotel, so I carried my suitcase there to save cab fare. Being unschooled in the need for advance travel arrangements, I simply walked up to the desk and asked for a room. After I paid, the receptionist gave me a key. Today, if someone walked into the main hotel of a major ECK seminar at the last minute, without a reservation, he might likely find himself without a room due to the thousands of people in attendance.

All four days I had the strong feeling that Paul would invite me for a consultation. Weeks before I left, the Inner Master — Paul's counterpart on the inner planes — had hinted at such a possibility. It never occurred to me that as the size of the ECKANKAR seminars grew, Paul would spend less time with each individual.

It was imperative to attend Paul's talks. Other than that, however, I roamed around the hotel, hoping to bump into him. He would naturally say, "Oh, Mr. Klemp, why don't you come up to my room for a minute." But that never happened.

I believe it was at this seminar that I wandered around like a lost sheep, not too particular about being anywhere on time. Paul's evening talk was scheduled to begin at a certain hour. Listless, I left my room late and made my way down to the large seminar room, which had been created with movable walls. By the time I arrived, Paul had begun his address. To my horror, the door was shut. A small crowd of other latecomers clustered around the doorway, until one of the men got up the courage to open the door and enter. An usher stopped him. "This door is closed. The Master is speaking." I was both crushed and humiliated, for one needed to show the highest respect for the Master. Tardiness, I then realized, was a mark of disrespect.

The small circle of people remained outside the locked door. A few others joined our group. Then it occurred to me that there must be another way into the seminar room, so I walked along the outside of the movable walls, looking for that place. On the far side, in the dark, was a place where the movable walls were not quite joined. It was possible to squeeze through an opening and enter the hall, then slip into an empty seat, which I could see just on the other side. I began to slip through the opening when a thought hit me: What kind of blessing can one expect if he disobeys the Master's wishes to sneak into the hall? With the chance to hear Paul right there, I returned instead to the first doorway and the crowd of latecomers.

Suddenly the door opened. "Paulji says you may come in and be seated," said the usher. Some of these people were so brazen as to waddle clear up the aisle to poke around for a front-row seat, while Paul glared at them from the stage. I was grateful just to be inside and quickly took a chair near the rear.

This experience taught me that respect for the Master is shown not only in words, but in one's behavior.

On Saturday I had the good fortune to be near one of the few Fifth Initiates of that time. The ECK movement was young, so those who made it to the Fifth Circle were looked upon almost as saints. Although that is often true spiritually, many initiates have a long way to go to bring their inner and outer lives into agreement. This Fifth Initiate was a doctor. I listened meekly as he spoke, because he was also on the Board of Trustees. He was one whom the Master relied upon to help shape the future of ECKANKAR. In addition, the doctor was an Initiator.

To me, the ECK initiations have always been a most sacred ritual. This means that whoever is to serve as

100

Initiator must purify his body and mind. He must bathe himself and adopt the highest state of detached love while performing this service as an instrument for the Mahanta. This care as to the sacredness of the initiation also extends to the gift which the initiate brings the Initiator as an offering of love for the Master.

A few minutes earlier, in an initiation ceremony, the doctor had received a love offering of two oranges. After the initiation, the Initiator came out into a small lobby on the mezzanine level and joined me on a couch. Looking around to see if anyone was watching, he set the fruit on the floor, abandoning it. To me, it showed a callous disregard for a gift of love intended for the Mahanta. Later, this doctor took up hypnotism in order to become an authority on past-life recall. This psychic diversion was not at all necessary. His daughter, also an ECKist, encouraged me to have a session with him to learn of my past lives. But from my viewpoint, hypnosis was at odds with the ECK teachings. If someone really wanted to know his past lives, the Mahanta recommended he learn the methods of the ECK-Vidya. And even these methods were only to be used to investigate one's own past, never that of another.

This was my first indication that just because a person carried the title of Mahdis, or Higher Initiate, it did not presume he was above a spiritual fall. Playing around with hypnosis as a means to study past lives showed that this individual was not as high in spiritual things as he supposed. But that was between him and the Master. I did nothing to cement a better friendship with this man, because our understanding of ECK was at odds. He was simply a product of the psychic awareness that was so strong during Paul's time. Paul catered to such people even though many of them were spiritually unstable. At least they were willing to search for the thread of ECK and perhaps follow it to the throne of God.

Truly feeling like a child in the wilderness, I wandered around the whole seminar trying to find an anchor point with someone.

Another time, I approached a group of young men standing in a circle around Tom Flamma. He was a dynamic initiate who had been a psychic healer before he came into ECK. In doing those healings, he had inadvertently taken on the karmic debts of other people: This came back upon him as a series of physical ailments. At one point, he came to an ECK seminar totally blind; and again, later, his vision was partially restored. Upon the occasion that he was blind, he nevertheless gave a talk. He walked upon the raised stage, microphone in hand, without any idea of where the edge of the stage dropped off to the floor. The audience was on the edge of their seats as he wandered near the dropoff, then away again—as if guided by the Inner Master. Whatever anyone might say of Tom, he was a colorful personality in the early days of ECKANKAR.

Now he stood surrounded by young men, each in the prime of life. I stood on the perimeter of the circle, happy to be near Tom, but also frightened that he might suddenly turn to me with a question I couldn't answer. He was known for that.

Then he said, "One of you standing here will become the Mahanta, the Living ECK Master."

His statement had come without preamble. Everyone was taken aback. The men looked at each other, then crowded closer to him to learn more of this great future that Tom foresaw for one of them. Looking at the competition, I stepped away from the group and went my own way. It would not be until the ECK Worldwide Seminar in October 1970 that Paul would open the

ECK-Vidya for me as he talked on stage, revealing that I was in training to be his successor.

Sunday morning came and still no word from Paul about a consultation. Paul and the Board of Trustees had met that morning, and the doctor's daughter was allowed to sit in on the meeting. On the table in the boardroom was a vase with twelve roses. Paul gave a rose to each of the people in the room, including the daughter. As I was leaving for the bus station after Paul's Sunday morning talk, she met me in the hallway and handed me the flower. "This is a gift from Paul," she said. Earlier, I had told her father and her that the Inner Master had promised a meeting that weekend. The rose was the Master's gift given through the agency of another person.

I took the flower and headed for the bus station. It was time to return to Wisconsin and my new proofreading duties. She also was taking a bus, so we went to the station together.

The rose from Paul had a strange effect upon me. An unfamiliar feeling of love began to enter my heart. Even though I thought I knew what ECK was all about, it had never occurred to me that It might be divine love—not Soul Travel.

She had several heavy suitcases. In addition to my own luggage, I was loaded down like a mule as we trudged down the street to the bus station. Farm work had made me strong, but even at that I was beginning to tire. As we descended the steps into the station, a rough-looking man came up the steps from below. Suddenly, he stopped and said to me, "You're not man enough for her."

Romance was not on my mind. I loved Paul, for he represented the reality of God's love for me. But this encounter marked the first time that I began to get an

103

inkling of the Golden-tongued Wisdom, the God-knowledge of the ECK-Vidya. That is the ancient science of prophecy. I thought I heard the ECK speaking to me through him. There seemed to be a deeper meaning in what this man said, so with my eyes shining, I set down the bags. Facing him, I said earnestly, "What did you say?"

It never occurred to me that my crouched stance might give him an impression of menace. Of my strength, I was sure. Farm work had toughened my muscles, and I had naturally quick reflexes. But self-defense or aggression was as far removed from my mind as was romance.

Later I tried to picture myself as he might have seen me. He's coming up the steps, leaving the bus station. Coming down toward him are a young woman and a country hick. Being a street-wise person, he determines that the bumpkin is no match for her. So he blurts out, "You're not man enough for her." Whereupon the bumpkin sets down the suitcases, but remains in a crouch. His eyes are bright and shining as he asks in a low, controlled voice, "What did you say?" The hick looks rugged and maybe a little crazy—those shining eyes.

Whatever went through his head when I asked him what he meant, he put his back against the wall and stared at me with fright. In the next instant he bolted for the exit. Shrugging at his peculiar behavior, I put on my donkey load of baggage again and deposited them at her bus, said good-bye, and tracked down my own bus for home.

It was on this bus that I handed the rose to a cute granddaughter in the seat ahead of me. She was being a perfect angel. Then she saw the rose in my lapel, where I had put it while lugging the bags. Once she took it, she turned into a complete monster. Screaming and shouting, she kicked at her grandmother, who was at a loss to explain this sudden change in disposition. Had the Master's love brought about such a negative state of emotions in the child? Not the love itself, only the quantity of it. There was too much coming through at once, and it was burning her inwardly. This is what caused the reaction.

But at that time I didn't realize what had caused the problem. In a very short time, I would see another example of people being burned by a careless dispersal of the God energy. This time it would be a willful act on my part. As a willful act, it would also be a violation of spiritual law.

I settled back in my seat with a feeling of great love, but also of loneliness. Shutting my eyes, I let the events of the seminar run through my mind like an image projected upon a screen. Proofreading was a temporary job that would provide an income while the greater plans of ECK were set into motion, I thought. Whatever those greater plans might be, I had no idea.

Full of love, loneliness, and even a little smugness, I settled back into my seat for the long ride home.

The proofreaders had gone out of control because they were not prepared for the spiritual energy that had suddenly engulfed them.

12

Bedlam in the Proofroom

The Midwest Seminar of 1970 was over, and I returned home quite a different person from the one who had left for the seminar three days earlier.

Paul had promised on the inner planes that we would meet at the seminar. Since he had met me once or twice at previous seminars, I just took the privilege for granted. But the weekend passed without so much as a nod from him. Although let down, I felt a rich stirring in my heart, like a love gift: an entirely new feeling.

Two classes of people in ECK, which might be found anywhere, include those who obey the letter of the law and those who live by the spirit of love. Until now, I was an unwitting member of the first group—a literalist. A person of the mind, not of the heart. The Midwest Seminar, in retrospect, was a turning point that allowed me to switch from having only a mental command of the ECK teachings to a spiritual one.

Before that change began to occur, I had already enjoyed an uncanny ability to recall the place in *The Shariyat-Ki-Sugmad* where Paul had stated any given precept. The teachings of ECK had been an integral part of me from the first. No matter where Paul had mentioned a particular subject, I could quickly locate it in the ECK books or discourses. If Paul had said it, I could find it.

Throughout my early years in ECK, I had many colorful dream and Soul Travel adventures. To all appearances I was a good, balanced chela of ECK: certainly sincere. And could anyone say he loved the Mahanta more than I did? But if someone had pointed out how little I actually knew of spiritual love, I would have pooh-poohed the accusation—because I did love the SUGMAD, the ECK, and the Mahanta with all my being. Yet it was a narrow love. A confining love that separated the trinity of ECKANKAR from down-to-earth living. In short, it was a *feeling* spun from the dwarfish mind powers instead of *real love* from the Ocean of Love and Mercy.

This, then, was the raw material the Mahanta had to deal with. Centuries of dos and don'ts by society had developed a hard crust around me like a lobster's shell. A living Soul existed in that shell, but it would take more than pliers to get me out.

I unpacked after arriving home from the bus station but was too agitated by this strange, new flow of love burning inside me to stay in my room. A few hours of sunshine remained on that Sunday afternoon, so I decided to take a walk. Somewhere must be a person who needed to hear about the ECK. With that vague plan in mind, I buttoned my winter coat and set out to see to whom the ECK would lead me. The spring season was too young for the first robins, but sparrows chirped their busy little sermons on frozen, brown lawns. A day of tranquility. Soon the exercise of walking about and the awareness of the soon-to-be warmer weather had the desired effect of calming my agitation.

It seemed unlikely anyone would be out this late in the afternoon with whom to share my exuberance from the seminar. Most people were sealed inside warm cars; nobody was out for a walk. So I gave up hope of finding someone to talk with about ECK. At that moment, however, I came to a bridge that spanned a wide river. On the far end of the bridge stood a bridge tender's shack. A large, heavyset man on the other side of the shack rested his elbows on the bridge's railing, as he stared out silently over the water. It appeared that the Mahanta had found someone after all who might benefit from what I had learned the past weekend in Chicago.

The man greeted me as I approached. Cars, trucks, and an occasional motorcycle rumbled over the bridge, making conversation difficult.

Like a regular missionary, I made small talk until there was an opening to give my message to this human being lost in spiritual darkness. Thankfully, I had the grace not to deal out unfamiliar ECKANKAR terms like *vairag, krodha, ahankara,* and others. But he knew a missionary when he saw one: he'd been around.

At first this man spoke the language of an illiterate. A hale and hearty sort of person, he would have looked at home in a bar with a mug of beer in hand, belting out a drinking song in a roomful of drunks. Full of life, goodwill, and cheer, he gave every appearance of a good-time Charlie. Just the kind of man who could most profit from the ECK teachings. In a very studious way, I hinted at great, unrecognized truths so generously strewn about us like pearls. Of course, I was not so ungracious as to add, "As pearls before the swine."

For a while, he listened in polite silence to my half-baked utterances, but then he switched my attention to a man riding a motorcycle across the bridge. By means of indirect speech, he compared the man on his motorcycle to Soul riding the Sound Current of God. Man, by his own power, could walk or run a relatively short distance, but a powered vehicle permitted him to reach for distant, unexplored places. Just like Soul on the winds of God. It must be understood that the stranger spoke indirectly; therefore, an element of truth already had to be implanted in the mind of the listener in order to understand him. Later, I would know this remarkable language of truth as the Golden-tongued Wisdom, a part of the ECK-Vidya, ancient science of prophecy.

In no time at all, I came to marvel at this man's wisdom. He could make a matter-of-fact connection between truth and its appearance in everyday things. His face, broad and open, was set with dark eyes that looked benignly upon a spiritually played-out world, and his staggering insight made my own understanding of life appear to be of little account. So I kept still and listened. He could see my fervent desire for truth.

To all appearances he was only a simple-hearted, unschooled bridge tender, a man of rough language and brusque manner. But his words were the sweet, golden honey of God. Despite my wide knowledge about the outer scriptures of ECK, I now realized how little I actually knew of life itself.

The walk back to my room was a thoughtful one. Given a choice I would have made any sacrifice to travel with Paul, my spiritual mentor, even if he never addressed me once: the love of ECK would rub off just by being in his presence. But Paul wasn't here. Furthermore, there seemed not the remotest chance of ever traveling with him. So if not with Paul then perhaps with this stranger, who appeared more and more to be one of the unknown ECK Masters.

Thus heartened, I went to a neighborhood restaurant for supper. Later at home, I took in the stark, barren room and was overwhelmed by a terrible loneliness. As long as the sun shone, the emptiness was held at bay; but with the approach of dusk, the forces of night closed in to torment my sleep. If only something worthwhile might come of my life. The proofreading job was a temporary convenience; another job in another town would serve as well. All that was missing was a reason to leave, to head for a place that offered a brighter, more promising future.

Ironically, my woeful surroundings did fit me like a glove: I was exactly where I belonged. The outer barrenness was a perfect imitation of the emptiness within me. How could this be? Didn't the ECK provide one with everything necessary for a full, happy life? That had been my impression, but here was the ugly fact of this dismal room: a lumpy bed, a battered dresser, a wobbly chair, and no pictures to grace the walls. Stained grey curtains shielded the windows. A sad place to call home. To make matters worse, the landlady complained that my typing disturbed her other tenants. "No typing after eight," she ordered. That closed in my world even more, cutting off a vital creative outlet.

A long, sleepless night passed. Before the first light of dawn, I donned my bathrobe to trudge upstairs to the common bathroom. As usual, I could see my breath in the hall. Five of us roomed in the house, so in order to arrive at work on time, I got up before the others to use the bathroom. It had no shower, only a bathtub, so I made it a practice to bathe the previous evening after the others were in bed. Even that brought a scolding, since the thin, uninsulated walls gave the impression of a waterfall roaring inside the house. So the landlady warned against late baths, too.

"My other tenants have been here a long time," she said. "I have to think about them."

* * *

111

My new proofreading job was a month old. This meant several cashed paychecks, but the bus trip to the ECK seminar in Chicago had pretty much cleaned me out. The soonest I could hope to move to a better place was a few months hence. A decided advantage to this location, however, was that it was within walking distance of my job, which would allow me to save for a car. In the meantime, I put up with long, cold walks to and from the publishing company every day. On alternate weeks, I was assigned to the evening shift. This meant a walk home at midnight—come blizzard, sleet, or rain.

This was my first day at work since the ECK seminar. Before being hired a month ago, I'd made it a condition to be allowed the Friday off to attend the Midwest Seminar. Of course, this raised questions about ECKANKAR. Hearing about Soul Travel upset several of my co-workers, as they tried to fit me into their predetermined codes of belief. Soul Travel, we know, is more than whizzing out of the body to some spiritual kingdom: a limited conception of it. Soul Travel is the movement of consciousness into a higher state of being. Often only a dim perception of Soul Travel remains upon awakening, leaving the person wondering if Soul Travel is scarcely more than a flight of fancy.

Soul Travel varies. It may actually be a startling movement of Soul from the human body. This usually occurs during sleep or contemplation, the sacred occasion when an ECKist practices the Spiritual Exercises of ECK, which link him to the Holy Spirit of Truth.

The proofreading room was large; windows overlooked the desks on two sides of the room. Special proofreading desks were set along the walls and also grouped in the middle of the room. A second room lay beyond the supervisor's desk, which was so placed that the supervisor could train a watchful eye on employees in either room. It was a few minutes before starting time. Proofreaders chatted in the hushed tones of morning drowsiness. Drinking coffee and nibbling on doughnuts, they looked curiously at the packets of reading material brought to them by the assistant supervisor. The packets constituted our morning's work.

Karen, my trainer, was already at the desk we shared. The best proofreader in the house, she was perhaps thirty, a detail person: an ideal trainer for new proofreaders.

As I drew my chair up to the desk and prepared to work, she asked, "How was your weekend?"

Curious about ECK, she was first and foremost a single woman raising a thirteen-year-old boy: a woman who wanted stability, both for herself and her son. Therefore, her curiosity about ECK was tempered with caution. I gave a quick summary of the weekend in Chicago, while the supervisor threw us warning looks: Work, don't talk. But every few minutes Karen asked more about ECK, and the interruptions were riding my nerves.

The reason for my annoyance was this: something unusual had happened to me in Chicago which I was at a loss to comprehend. It concerned the experience of divine love. The Mahanta's love had touched me over the weekend, but I couldn't put it into perspective. All I knew for certain was that a feeling of great love now sometimes filled me. This indefinable feeling of love had grown until it was no longer just a feeling, but a force as real as water rushing down a river. It was simply the divine energy of life. I knew it mentally, but now I had to learn to accept this Spirit of Love in every waking moment.

Bent over the assignment at my desk, I suddenly was out of my body. As Soul, I was on the ceiling, on the other side of the room—all at my pleasure. The force of divine love flowing into me like a stream of water was responsible for this Soul Travel experience in the proofroom. Tender love, bliss, ecstasy, goodwill, resting in the arms of God: all of these ideas poured through my mind as I tried to understand the beautiful language of love that carried me beyond the tedium of the mind and into the grandeur of spiritual bliss. The stream of divine love ran into me from a place above, pouring in like a column of Light.

This was a new experience. A state of detached bliss that still allowed me to work at the desk, to search in the dictionary, to make proofreading corrections, and to log my work—all the mundane things a proofreader needed to do for a paycheck. What a delightful enchantment, this current of God. For the first time, I knew the meaning of joy. A pure, simple joy beyond definition. There was no way to explain it to someone else, nor did I want to. It was a personal state of spiritual being that transported me into the blissful worlds of God.

A smile lit my face as my pencil passed over galley after galley. Karen became more determined than ever to learn the reason for my happiness.

ECKists often have a glow of light and love streaming from them for several days after an ECK seminar, according to observations made by their friends. This glow is the Sound and Light of God, the stream of love that flows between the Holy Spirit and an individual. The Sound and Light were present in me too—but many times stronger than ever before. During the midmorning break, several proofreaders approached to say that a light seemed to shine from me. What was it? Where had I been last weekend? What had I done? I was relieved when the fifteen-minute break ended so I could slip from my body to reenter the wonderful rapture of God.

Karen, however, wouldn't leave me alone. I now know that the energy that lifted me up was also felt by others. Feeling happy to the point of giddiness, they sought the source of their light-heartedness, and automatically looked in my direction. In the meantime Karen was actually burning inwardly from this energy, because she was not accustomed to it. In a way, she unconsciously tried to defuse it by pelting me with a barrage of questions. Every time she asked a question, it forced me to leave this column of Light and Sound, and return to my body to respond to her; this momentarily reduced the inner scorching. But soon my patience came to an end. I wanted to remain in that vertical stream of holy energy and not have to abandon it for every silly question.

When the noon bell rang, I retreated to the snack room upstairs, feeding coins into a vending machine for a can of soup and crackers. Few employees used the room. Most preferred to brown-bag their lunches; a few ran errands during the noon hour; and a couple of them enjoyed a restaurant meal. I chose the machine lunch, hardly aware of the bland food in my mouth.

Instead, I was electrified by the sweet current of God that passed through me from head to foot. What was It, this wonderful Sound and Light of God? It tingled through my body with a swishing sound, like a gentle river. Or it may have been a distant waterfall of pure white Light, enfolding me in arms of delightful rapture. My heart overflowed with waves of love, and I wished to give up all and follow the Mahanta to the ends of the earth, to the end of time.

A bell jangled, signaling the end of the lunch hour. Hurrying to my desk in the proofroom, I found Karen already poring over a galley. She shot me a reproachful look for returning late. But I was beyond ill will,

115

pettiness, and all other trifles. It was now obvious why those who receive the kiss of God no longer bump and scrape to the conventions so crucial to society. My body was like a machine, yet Soul was in perfect control of it. Obediently, my physical self picked up a pencil to correct a galley, while I—the Real Self—enjoyed the inexpressible love and joy of the Holy Spirit.

Karen leaned over to remind me of a technical detail about the copy I was proofing. Before lunch, I had made the mistake of hinting at this wonderful energy of God. Now she pressed me to talk about It. The supervisor cleared his throat from his desk, and other proof-readers shot looks our way. They thought romance was in the wind, but her interruptions were getting tiresome.

To counteract her continual interference, a thought came to mind: Why not redirect this God energy?

What a splendid idea! Until now, I had simply allowed the God energy to flow down through me, but the continual movement between the Soul and physical bodies caused by her questioning suggested an experiment. Rather than passively letting the flow go through me, I would redirect it into the proofroom. The idea offered a new dimension of experience. It did not occur to me that I was crossing the fine line between a God-directed individual and a black magician. A channel for God acts only as the Spirit of God directs him; a black magician attempts to bend the divine power to his own end.

Misuse of the God power is commonplace; it happens all the time. A channel for God says, "Thy will be done," but a black magician's invocation is quite different—"My will be done." Someone who sends a prayer to God to end a drought is actually saying, "O God, your decision to create this drought was wrong; it's time for rain." Such a person is an unconscious dabbler in the black arts. Prayer that directs God to act in a certain way is seldom recognized for the negative power that it is.

By attempting to direct the God Force, I was unwittingly breaking a spiritual law. I had very clearly felt the energy of Spirit flow into me from above, but where it went after that wasn't a concern. Until now. Now, I decided, it should flood the proofroom. How would the proofreaders respond to this invisible, but powerful, energy when it swept over them like a flood tide? An interesting experiment.

The mechanics of how this God Stream can be manipulated by an adjustment to one's attitude is too hard to explain. Suffice it to say, it can be done.

The building had an air-conditioner, but on warm days — like that afternoon — the proofreaders were allowed to open windows so that the pleasant air of spring might enter the room. Until now, except for Karen's whispered probings, our union shop had been relatively peaceful. Proofreaders worked quietly. The only sounds were low conversations or the swishing of pages being turned. The proofroom was as hushed as a library.

Then I began to bend this stream of divine energy into the room. Like a fireman aiming a hose, I directed this flow into the proofroom. Almost immediately came a reaction.

Staid proofreaders began to act like spoiled brats. Dan, who wanted to work in radio someday but had taken this job to buy a car, made a paper airplane and sailed it across the room. Linda, a pretty but petulant young woman, picked it up from the floor and flung it back. Jack snapped a spitball that zinged Helen on the neck. A less inventive proofreader, who wanted in on

117

the fun, began to toss paper clips at random. Then Margaret spilled her coffee, which left a brown puddle on a page proof. Meanwhile, our dignified supervisor began to clear his throat with ever-louder ahems. He'd lost control of his staff.

While bedlam reigned, I behaved like a perfect angel. The supervisor was making mental notes of the troublemakers, which would later influence raises and promotions. Why risk my future?

Then an inner voice thundered, "Enough!" It was surprisingly like the voice of the bridge tender. Anyway, I had grown tired of this game. It was fun only so long to watch adults act like children; the novelty of this experiment had passed. Obediently, I shut down the invisible valve that opened into the room. Just that quickly order was restored. The supervisor harrumphed to reestablish the dignity of his office as he made the rounds. "It's time we got back to work, don't you think?"

Why had the proofreaders gone out of control? They simply were not prepared for the spiritual energy that had suddenly engulfed them. These divine energies are real. They will burn those who are not conditioned through the Spiritual Exercises of ECK to receive them.

Without any awareness of it, I had breached the spiritual Law of Noninterference.

"What do you think God Consciousness is?" said the stranger, turning back to the railing.

13

A Sharp Rebuke

After work, I went to the neighborhood restaurant for supper. What a day! The bedlam in the proofroom did cause some uneasy moments: a lesson overlooked? Whatever it was, I couldn't place it.

The coldness of my room in that uninviting house was offensive, so I took a walk. My feet seemed to have a homing device built into them, because they bore me straight to the bridge again. The stranger was outside his hut as before, leaning over the rail. He glanced my way as I approached from the far side of the bridge, but then he returned to look at the river. I greeted him in the friendly but reserved manner of a midwesterner. He acknowledged my greeting, but tonight there was a raw chill in his voice. It felt like the coolness between friends when one has offended the other.

"The God Force is an impartial current of energy," he said. "Like the electricity that runs through the wires in your room, it can light a lamp or heat a meal. But it can also be an instrument of destruction should the wire that conducts it become frayed or shorted out."

Wonderful! The stranger was giving a classic discourse on God. Outside of Paul and the ECK Masters, he was the only person I'd met who could speak in such concise terms about the truth behind life.

Slowly he turned to face me. Yesterday he had seemed like nothing more than a jovial but unlettered laborer, but today his eyes blazed like darts of lightning. No doubt, this would be an exceptional discourse.

"Today you burned innocent people through a misuse of the God Power," he said.

The stranger, his shack, the bridge—all began to swim before my eyes. A powerful current of energy swirled around him, a current so dynamic that I could barely keep to my feet. And with it came a terrible feeling that I was a wretch on trial for a horrible crime.

"You burned people," he said. "As surely as spilling hot coffee on them, you burned them."

At a loss for words, I searched his face for an explanation. This was not the discourse I had expected to hear: great truths about God and life. Instead, a sharp rebuke. Confused, I stammered, "But I didn't know."

"An ECK Master is a God-directed being," said the stranger. "He never begs off his folly behind a skirt of ignorance. What do you think God Consciousness is?" The stranger returned to the railing, his back to me.

My ears burned with shame. It wasn't only what he said outwardly that dismayed me, but also what came through the inner channels. As an ECK initiate, I had been entrusted with a spiritual power hundreds of times greater than anything my co-workers in the proofroom could ever have imagined. With that trust came an obligation not to abuse it. Ironically, the spiritual law that applied to this spiritual power was not spelled out to me before the power was placed in my hands. It was like allowing a small child to drive a truck on the freeway.

122

"This time I took the punishment for the burn," he said, turning his stern face toward me again. "Next time, it's yours."

The bridge tender disappeared into his shack without a backward glance. I stared miserably at the closed door, slowly realizing the awful responsibility that accompanied the God Power.

But how could I know what I didn't know? I asked myself. A Catch-22 situation.

The Order of Vairagi Adepts tests an individual many times before he is allowed into the secret brotherhood. The ECK Masters waste no time on fools. Had my misuse of the God Power destroyed my chance at God-Realization? It seemed so. Dreading the coming night, I feared tomorrow even more.

From out of the night came a searing bolt of blue-white light that pierced my heart.

14

The Experience of God

What is life without the experience of God? There are many misconceptions about God-Realization, and I had most of them. One is that the individual who has been to the SUGMAD sees all, knows all. While this is true in part, he sees and knows only what he must in order to survive, in any world, at any time.

In *The Tiger's Fang,* Rebazar Tarzs has just returned from taking Peddar Zaskq to the SUGMAD. They are sitting alongside a rocky trail in a frozen wilderness when the great ECK Master Shamus-i-Tabriz rides up on a camel. Rebazar greets him and says, "We have been to the SUGMAD." Shamus-i-Tabriz looks at Peddar Zaskq and asks, "He has become the Anami? Then he should know all things, but I see by the light around him there are many things yet that he needs to know before being accepted into the ancient order of the Bourchakoun!"

The experience of God will certainly transform the thoughts, feelings, and behavior of anyone, but weeks or months may pass before he reestablishes himself in society. The individual with true God-Realization is

125

suddenly out of key with social conventions, yet he eventually discovers that to serve the SUGMAD may mean enduring life among the spiritually dead—Souls with darkened lamps. God-Realization may span from a profoundly beautiful experience to the ruthless tearing away of one's final illusions.

This turning point of all my lives occurred that second night on the bridge where I met the stranger. My search for God had run the ages, though I had on occasion managed to touch His fleeting garments. But I was left then to weep alone in the wilderness of longing, victim of my craving hunger. A child in spiritual things, I sought the secret of the Sound and Light, the two aspects by which God is known to man. All of this was to come that night on the bridge, leaving me forever changed in heart, body, mind, and Soul.

The 1970 Midwest Seminar in Chicago with Paul Twitchell had been over since noon on Sunday; it was the following Tuesday night. I sat alone in my dismal room in the house with paper-thin walls, wanting to tell someone of my love for the Mahanta, of which I had become painfully aware over the weekend. The landlady's strict rule of no typing after eight o'clock in the evening put a damper on my habit of corresponding with friends, which was a way of talking out my thoughts. No radio or television, and the room was cold. She kept the temperature down in order to help pay the expenses for a yearly trip to Phoenix—where indeed she was even now—while in our rooms the other boarders and I shivered in flannel shirts and robes.

It was spring. I pushed the moth-eaten curtain aside for a look at the chilly, damp street lit by an occasional dim streetlight. My loneliness was so compelling that I decided to chance the night chill and go for a walk toward the river, as I had the night before.

Moving past the narrow space between my bed and dresser, I heard the musical laughter of Cathy, the landlady's teenage daughter, chime through the wall. She and a girlfriend were on the phone discussing boys at school. I shrugged, pulled my overcoat from a hanger in the closet, and stepped out into the dark cold.

My heels clicked along the pavement at a steady pace. The memory of Paul at the seminar was still fresh. On the inner he had said he would meet me there, but never did. Was the Mahanta telling me to put more reliance upon the Inner Master?

Near the river was a tavern. Through the window I could see it was empty except for the bartender, so I went in to escape the cold and perhaps strike up a conversation.

When I ordered, he raised his eyebrows and repeated, "Club soda?" He shook his head but squirted carbonated water from a spigot into a glass. A teenage girl came in to ask for change, which he hurriedly gave her, mindful of the law prohibiting minors in a bar. While wiping up imaginary water spots on the bar, he asked, "Are you a minister?"

"Why?"

"Because you sound like one." I was offended, but shared a little of my interest in religion.

Then a strange thing happened: the ECK-Vidya, or the Golden-tongued Wisdom, came from his lips. This is the God language, the ancient science of prophecy. He was not aware of it, but the Mahanta was using him to give my future by this indirect manner of speech.

He said that before the night was out I would face a challenge so dreadful that nothing in my past could compare with it. No matter what was said for me to do, it must be done instantly, with complete faith in the Mahanta. Further, I would ride in an ambulance before the sun rose in the morning.

"Go to another town," he warned. "Don't let them take you to our hospital. An engine will be switching freight cars and block the tracks. Just when you'll need help fast."

His warnings shook me. So I said good night and returned to my room. Next door, Cathy was still laughing on the phone. My room beckoned like a cell, barring even the simplest happiness. I shuddered, rebuttoned my overcoat, and took another walk. A while later, when I emerged from my thoughts, I was surprised to be alongside the bridge. On the far side, golden beams of light streamed from the windows of the bridge tender's shack.

I still chafed at the stranger's tongue-lashing of the previous night. He said I had burned people. Nevertheless, there was a compulsion to return to his shack, perhaps because it seemed to be a sort of way station on the road to God. Yet my fear of him made me consider whether I might slip past without his notice. But a greeting boomed from the shack.

"I wondered if you had the guts to come back," he said from the open doorway.

For the next half hour, he spoke about the Sound and Light, and the Presence of God. While he spoke, a high humming sound played at the rim of my consciousness. A warm blanket of love shielded me from the shivering cold that reached for my bones. Just before midnight, the tone of his voice changed abruptly.

"Are you ready to meet yourself?" he asked gently, shedding the rough-and-tumble language of an illiterate laborer.

I gave a mute nod. The Golden-tongued Wisdom from earlier this evening now flooded across my mind: Accept all that comes tonight, without fear or hesitation. Thus began my rite of passage into God-Realization.

The stranger studied me. "Are you ready to face the Mountain of Yama?"

The Mountain of Yama? I listened in disbelief. The mountain of death? Though shaking with fear, I nodded. Until now, when the stranger spoke of Yama, I could have convinced myself that his wisdom, given in doublespeak, was simply my delusion. However, the phrase "Mountain of Yama" was known to few, even in ECKANKAR. But it had always carried a special attraction for me. So when the stranger used it, he gave me the first real indication of this meeting's importance.

Rebazar Tarzs once said, "Only the bold and adventuresome find God." Might that include giving up one's life? I hoped not. The thought of death turned my blood to ice.

The stranger broke in on my thoughts.

"Look there!" he said. "The Light of God!" From out of the night, as if from a distant lighthouse, came a searing bolt of blue-white light that pierced my heart. He smiled. "The Light of God; It shines for thee."

He cocked his head, listening. His eyes lit with joy, and he turned to me. "Listen! The Sound!"

A heavy roll of thunder shook the bridge, as if a locomotive were sweeping past a railroad crossing at high speed. I trembled at the power of the sound.

The stranger gave a quiet laugh. "Behold! The Light and Sound of God."

All became still. The sound of thunder ceased, but the Light of God poured endlessly into my heart as It swept down from the God planes, from the very center of all creation—the SUGMAD. No thoughts stirred inside me. I was at peace, untroubled even by the possible specter of death, and waited quietly—but for what?

"Contemplate upon the Sound and Light of God," said the bridge tender, and he disappeared into his shack.

For my part, a calming hand seemed to hold me in its tender grasp. I faced the river waters, looking out toward the beam of searing light, standing quietly as if frozen in place. For a while, all was still. No cars rattled over the bridge at this hour; no pedestrians disturbed my vigil. Still I waited, wondering, What more could this stranger want of me?

Then it came, barely a breath of sound gliding over the water. Puzzled, I listened, head cocked. The soft ripple of sound washed in again. Without a doubt, it was ocean waves upon a peaceful shore. How could that be? This was a river, a dirty city river, whose hushed waters hardly rippled as they flowed lazily between its concrete banks.

The sound of waves grew still. A pause, then again the ocean swell, but this time more compelling. A stilling, then another rushing.

The tide must be coming in, I thought. Faster, louder came the surging. Thunderous, booming, crashing.

"O God, no!" I cried. With each tidefall, I reeled. The full Ocean of Love and Mercy was crushing me, cleansing, scouring, blessing. A great pain burst through me: a white-hot fire. I screamed in agony, "O God, let this stop!" But the waters of life kept washing, churning, boiling.

The Sound was All. It filled my every atom. The sweet and holy Current of God cradled me with Its fierce love. There was no part of me where It was not.

This was ECK, the ancient, ageless, Voice of God, giving new life to Its creation. The celestial Sound and Light of God swept over, through, and from me. Long cries of anguish rose from my depths, deep and full. My body was ripped, slashed by a thousand claws, and as many hammers pounded from all sides.

I then became aware of standing bent over double on the bridge. Ghastly screams rent the night. Was this me? Suddenly I was in the Atma Sarup, at a distance, watching as ages of karma were ripped from me at once. Illusions must all be gone before Soul may tread the hallowed grounds of the One Most High.

Finally, the crashing waves from the Ocean of Love and Mercy began to wane. Slowly I straightened up. My sides burned with a stabbing pain, from the screams that came with Soul's cleansing. But my atoms were pure and light beyond all telling. A disease was now gone, but until its absence, I had not even sensed its presence.

"Something's gone," I murmured. "Something's gone."

A heaviness that had been with me all my years was gone.

Freedom. Was this spiritual liberation? If so, to what could it compare? Who else knew of its lightness? Who else could understand this freedom? I was airy in my atoms, like a child afloat on water. Something had gone indeed: my karma, the heavy hand of destiny.

The strength of God now rushed through me. I would give up all to serve the SUGMAD. What other reason was there for life?

The stranger stepped from his shack. "The blessings of the Ancient One be with you."

Like an orphaned duckling in search of a new mother, I thought, let me serve this stranger. But like the duckling that nearly chose a fox, I also had to choose more wisely. Next to learn was that Soul's service can only be to God alone. Within moments, this stranger was to teach me a harsh lesson of self-reliance.

Though having seen the face of God, I, like Paul, still had so much to learn. And was still, a child in the wilderness.

In the snap of a finger, the stranger changed from the noble ECK Master, who had taken me to the SUGMAD, to an outraged and spiteful laborer tending a bridge.

15

A Bitter Lesson on Self-Reliance

The experience of God was fresh, and my love for the SUGMAD all-embracing. Like a bridegroom refreshed by his bride's adoring love, I wished to bathe forever in the bliss of God.

Slowly I took stock of the night around me. The Sound and Light were gone; only the shack and the bridge remained, and the river. The door to the shack was thrust open and the bridge tender stepped out.

"Tell me what you saw," he said.

"There is only the Light and Sound of God," I replied. A smile traced the corners of his mouth.

"Then return to the world and serve the SUGMAD," he said.

I shook my head. "I want to go with you."

The stranger pulled back, scowling. "All who see the Ultimate must serve It evermore. Go now and learn your mission."

My vision of what it meant to serve God was like that of many others: wander at will, shun responsibility, and appear saintly.

The stranger grunted in disgust. "Listen, the road to God never ends. However hard you found it, the easy

135

part is in getting to the Ocean of Love and Mercy. Serving people in all their states of slumber takes more patience than befits a saint. ECK Adepts don't waste their lives in idle contemplation."

"Teach me the wisdom of God," I begged.

In the snap of a finger, the stranger changed from the noble ECK Master, who had taken me to the SUGMAD, to an outraged and spiteful laborer tending a bridge.

"What's a matter with you?" he shouted. "You some kinda jerk? Get away!"

Stunned by this outburst of rage from the man who had spoken of the Mountain of Yama, and who had given me the experience of God, I said meekly, "Take me with you." He spit on the pavement in front of me.

In a moment I was also to see the hideous god of light: the Kal Niranjan in the guise of Paul. A strong feeling inside me said Paul was near, that he and this stranger were friends. Surely the bridge tender wouldn't send me away. Wasn't his rudeness just a test of my faith in the Mahanta, who then was Paul? The bridge tender strode back and forth outside the shack, barely containing his anger. He peered toward a shadowy street at the end of the bridge, as if expecting company.

Then from the shadows walked a smallish man. He wore no winter coat, only a long-sleeved blue shirt and trousers of the same color. His clothes were much too thin for a cold, damp night like this. My heart leaped with joy as the man came closer. That's Paul! I thought. But when light from the window fell upon him, I recoiled in horror. It revealed a face scarred and cruel, the most evil-looking mockery of Paul that one could imagine.

My mind spun back to the Midwest Seminar in Chicago. Two photos of Paul were on display in the bookroom: the first showed a genial Paul with a wan smile; the second pose showed him with a Soul-tearing frown. This man on the bridge, a parody of Paul, was a grotesque imitation of Paul's second photo. For a moment I debated whether the real meaning of "The Two Faces of the Master" was to suggest a parallel to the Old Testament God of anger vs the New Testament's God of love. Of course, I knew there was no parallel here between ECK and Christianity. "The Two Faces" simply referred to the spiritual duties of the Outer and Inner Master in ECK.

"Who's your buddy?" the man in blue asked my stranger.

"No friend a mine," said the bridge tender. "He's some kinda jerk."

Chirping at just the wrong time, like a young sparrow fallen from its nest, I peeped, "Take me with you, Paul."

"What's that?" asked the man in blue. He measured me up and down with a critical eye. The bridge tender said, "He wants to go with us. What do you think about that?" The man in blue, in fact, did have an opinion: He laced the night with a stream of profanity. It felt like being hit by a lightning storm.

The overwhelming encounter with God's Sound and Light had left me in a daze of rapture that clashed violently with this dark world. The sudden shift in the bridge tender's posture from inspiration to malice baffled me. First, I was his comrade; then, an outcast. But unknown to me at the time, he was teaching a bitter lesson on self-reliance, a quality that marks every ECK Master.

How many luckless individuals get lost in meditation by trying to recapture the ecstasy of God when they should now be serving the Deity? Unless an ECK Master is nearby to help them reenter this world, they risk stagnation in their spiritual lives. Proud to have reached the summit of heaven, they have but tripped on a foothill of God's mountain.

The bridge tender switched off the lights in his shack. A dull street lamp on each end of the bridge cast a dim light as he locked the door. The two men started for a parking lot at the far end of the bridge, with me trailing along behind them.

"Get away!" hissed the man in blue. A hideous scar on his left cheek twisted like a dagger when he spoke. In my state of imbalance, I thought: The Mahanta is in everybody—this must be Paul! Like so many other truth seekers, I did not understand that the Mahanta was always a clear channel for ECK, and that ordinary people could only communicate the ECK message with lesser degrees of reliability. It was not the Mahanta, or Paul, who spoke through the man in blue, but his adversary: Kal Niranjan, king of the negative worlds.

Bewildered, I stopped to let them go. Then the bridge tender turned to me and said in a candid tone, "Remember the Mountain of Yama." That set me off again. His sudden utterance threw me back to ground zero—spiritually everywhere, but nowhere. I trailed behind them across the bridge to their car, like a beggar asking alms from beggars. The men stopped beside an old two-door car and began to climb in. Like a whimpering child, I cried, "Take me with you."

The man in blue reached behind the right front seat and produced an enormous wrench. Malice darkened his face. He gripped the weapon in his right hand and said, "Beat it or I'll bust you!"

With reason on his side, I backed up to give him plenty of room. The overwhelming experience on the bridge had left me in a state of imbalance, but not completely robbed of my senses. He shook the wrench once more, to keep me at bay, then jumped into the passenger's seat and locked his door. The stranger turned the key, and the engine coughed awake in the cold night. The car's backup lights glared in my face as the car shot into reverse, barely missing me. The driver jammed the accelerator, spinning the car in a half circle. The tires spit gravel at the wooden guardrail that kept parked cars from rolling into the river. As the car sped into the dark, I caught a final glimpse of the bridge tender hunched over the steering wheel.

The mountain of death, I thought. Why did he say, "The Mountain of Yama"? In my bewildered state, I was to carry this remarkable night of experience a step too far.

As I pulled myself along, hand over hand, toward the shore, I gave thanks for life.

16

In Cold, Dark Waters

Nothing made sense. The experience of God should make one happy, light, and free. Was that always true? For here I was at the side of a river, in the cold darkness of winter, forsaken and alone. Where was the joy? What good was God-Realization if it left those who had it in a condition like mine?

The wisdom of God had been given to me through a baptism of Sound and Light. They had ripped me apart, then put me back together after a fashion. There was a difference in my thinking and feeling, of this there was no doubt. Not the outer side, but inwardly. A lightness buoyed me up, in spite of this sordid midnight setting. All in all, I felt the fullness of all that is good. It was unlike any joy I had ever felt before; therefore, I was hard put to call it "joy." The Sound and Light had given me a rich, deep happiness that did not depend upon outer conditions. Heaven knows, nothing around me could evoke mirth.

Contradictions boiled within me: I was joyous, yet pathetic; light, but melancholy; free, yet not free.

Far down the street, where the two strangers had disappeared in their car, a set of headlights swung around the corner. A car roared through the night toward me. I edged closer to the guardrail. Earlier, the stranger had nearly backed over me when he left the parking lot in such a hurry.

The car came fast. Right opposite the parking lot, the driver squealed the brakes and stopped. It was the two men again. This time I stayed put. They took a long look, then swung the car back in the direction it had come. Again I was alone with the night. Their return was a reminder. The stranger had said, "Are you ready to face the Mountain of Yama?" He had given a second reminder on the bridge, after his pal had come. They had started for the car when the stranger turned to me and said, "Remember the Mountain of Yama." Their brief return was a third reminder of a task unfinished.

Now I recalled something the stranger had said the previous night. He had been speaking in the Golden-tongued Wisdom of the ECK-Vidya. In the trunk of his car, he said, was a long electrical cord. "What do you carry that for?" I asked. Pointing to the river, he replied, "In case somebody falls in, I can pull him out." In an odd sort of way that seemed to be a lot of foresight. My mind began to put these bits and pieces of information together: Mountain of Yama, and a lifeline. It was suddenly plain what had to be done next. I had to face my fear of death by jumping into the river.

It is easy to say, A clear-cut case of delusion; or madness, brought on by too much stress. That is an easy way out. Before this experience was over, I would realize firsthand why some people commit suicide: to please a tyrannical God. They love God so much that they are willing to sacrifice their lives for Him. As off-beam as they might be in their thinking, there is still a sort of honesty to it. Most of us would certainly not copy their behavior. It is enough to understand their thinking when they go off and do such spiritual harm to themselves.

Across the river, two men sat on a factory dock. Their voices carried easily across the water. They were on the midnight shift. Work rules were more lax there, perhaps as an unofficial apology from the company to its workers for keeping them from their families at night.

Beyond the guardrail, two ducks made ripples in the river. They had swum out to deeper water when I disturbed them at the car's approach. It was easy to spot them in the light cast from the dock beyond the river, where the men had turned on a spotlight. Now the ducks came to shore again. Yama, lifeline, swimming ducks. All the pieces fell into place. The final test, I thought, was to face my fear of death. It meant jumping into the river and swimming out again, like the ducks. No doubt the stranger was keeping a vigil over me from his car, parked nearby in the dark. He would lug the extension cord with him to rescue me. Of course! It all fit.

What was there to fear? If I jumped in, surely he and his buddy in blue would fish me out. And I would have passed the age-old test: defeating the fear of death.

So perfect. Even though I felt a need to fulfill the last phase of this night of testing, I was not going to lose my head about it. There seemed to be leeway in choosing where to jump into the river, in the middle or near the side. A jump from the middle of the bridge was bucking the odds. What if the stranger did not show up? To me, the problem was not unlike baptism. Some Christians feel that a true baptism can only be achieved by total immersion. Others, like the Lutherans, are content to dip a cloth into a bowl of water and simply sprinkle the infant's head. Each rite of baptism is sacred in its respective church.

143

Likewise, it seemed, the final test of God-Realization demanded a plunge. No matter if this was early spring, with blocks of ice still adrift in the water. Had I been of Baptist upbringing, I might have chosen the middle of the bridge, to do the job right. But I was from Lutheran stock. So I made a survey of the best place to carry out the jump. Being of a practical Lutheran bent, it seemed least chancy to jump in near shore, where the water must be shallow.

The stranger's car was not anywhere in sight: No harm in looking for a last-minute deliverance. "You have done well, my son," the stranger would say as he gave me permission to step down from the guardrail, where I'd be perched, ready to scare the ducks out of their wits with a cannonball splash. In parting the stranger would say, "Purity of heart and love for God have vanquished all your fear, even that of death. Depart in peace." And I would depart right then.

That was my dream, but no one came. The two workmen across the river got up to go inside the factory. They changed their minds and stopped for a last smoke.

What point was there in putting this test off any longer? Shaking, I climbed onto the guardrail and looked into the cold, black waters. The ducks looked up sleepily at me, then rustled awake to head offshore. Just in case. My wallet bulged in my left hip pocket. Too bad, in a second my money and identification papers would be drenched. Oh well, who said the path to God was easy? For that matter, the water wouldn't do much for my shoes either, which already squeaked.

Certain of rescue, I pulled my overcoat tightly around me and jumped six feet through the air and hit the icy water. My landing made a big whump. Just as I cleared my ears and began to swim for my life, one of the men on the dock exclaimed, "What was that?" Both

144

listened in silence, while I did my best to swim to shore as quietly as possible.

"Whatever it was, it's gone now," said a voice. "Let's go in."

The current was sweeping me slowly downstream. My soaked clothing made it nearly impossible to stay afloat. The view from the water was quite different than from the bridge. A serious problem faced me: The shoreline had been braced with a wall of concrete and planking to prevent dirt from spilling into the river. The shoring had a five-foot rise from the water to the top of the wall. How was I to get out? Panic began to set in. Fear of death was not at work now, but a fear of failure.

As I treaded water, moving closer to shore, I was relieved to feel the bottom under my feet. Exposure to the arctic water might soon bring death, but for the moment, the likelihood of death by drowning was out of the picture. Now what?

Then I saw the lifeline. It was not the extension cord stored in the stranger's trunk, but a cable used to anchor a light pole set at the edge of the parking lot. Utility workers had run a cable from the middle of the pole and anchored it in the water. The cable was slack; the anchor had pulled loose from the river bottom. It seemed a strange place to fasten a cable, but there it was. Swimming toward it, I pulled myself along, hand over hand, toward the shoring. The slack in the cable was just enough to allow me to pull myself up the wall and catch hold of the guardrail. Panting, I gave thanks for life.

The ducks remained halfway across the river. How were they to rest with people doing cannonballs into their watery bed?

My breath steamed white against the night air. My room was a long eight blocks away. The bars were closing, and cars appeared on the streets as patrons drove home. My path home meant passing a row of taverns, because the cold required the quickest route. Pneumonia was a real concern.

Wet shoes make a funny sloshing sound. I left the parking lot, wished it good riddance, and headed home along the sidewalk. Ever so often, I looked back at the peculiar water trail behind me. To all appearances, a big fish had left the river for a midnight stroll in town. The sidewalk was a blotch of water stains. My route required passing a well-lighted bar, and when I was past its entrance, safe again in the dark, two inebriated men lurched out of the door. They stopped, puzzled at the trail of water on the pavement. The whites of their eyes grew large as they peered up and down the street, at each other, then hastily crawled into a car in front of the tavern. Neither spoke.

I slipped behind a tree as their car inched into the street. Two silent, slack-faced men, their eyes riveted on the road ahead, ruminating on mischief wrought by the demon rum.

I was shivering. The lights were out in the house when I returned to my room. Cathy had finished talking with her friend. The other roomers were all asleep. I sloshed into the house through my private entrance. This would be the time to soak in a hot bath, except for yet another house rule: No baths after ten o'clock. Maybe a flannel shirt and bathrobe would stop this shaking.

By now I was shivering violently. But shortly I'd be in bed. A little while longer, in the world of dreams. The restful cloud of unknowing.

In spite of having had the experience of God, I felt no elation. There was no exaltation, no longer any ecstasy. I was cold. Tired. Yet, the night had more in store for

146

me. My fear of the mountain of death was history, but life held more terrors than could be rinsed off with one dip in a river. On the verge of exhaustion, I had overlooked the Golden-tongued Wisdom that the Mahanta had given earlier this night through the bartender: "Before the night is over, you will be taken in an ambulance."

Now I yearned for sleep. First rubbing myself vigorously with a bath towel in a vain attempt to restore warmth to my frozen limbs, I slid under the covers. And the rest of the night began.

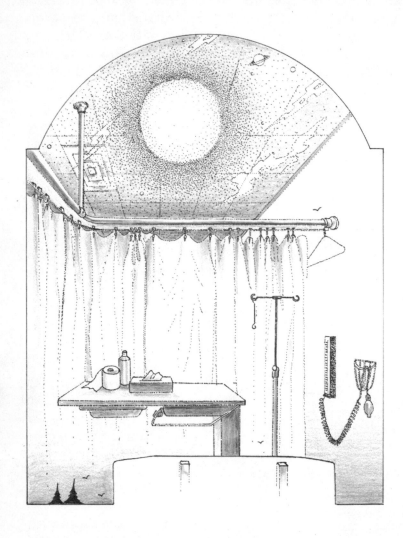

With the Blue Light came a warmth that reached to
my bones, warming the chill of my wild shivering.

17

Blue Light of the Mahanta

Little more than two hours ago the grace of the SUGMAD had come upon me in the experience of God-Realization. By now all should have been bliss in my worlds, but that was far from true. As I got into bed, my thoughts were on Paul Twitchell, who was the Mahanta, the Living ECK Master.

My body shivered violently under the covers. A bath in the icy river near midnight had been a terrible shock. If only there were a way to get warm. I put on flannel pajamas and pulled a heavy bathrobe over them, my winter coat on top of both. In bed, I drew the patched sheet and woolen blanket over my head to warm the air under the covers with breathing. Anything for warmth. Next door, Cathy, the landlady's daughter, was up and about again, not able to sleep. There was the clunk of a kettle being set on the stove, to brew herself a cup of coffee.

What was it that Rebazar Tarzs, the Tibetan ECK Master, had said to Paul about God-Realization in *Stranger by the River?* His words, which I later checked, were these: "It is always possible to see God. But you must do as I say; repeat the sacred names, and do all

149

thy work in ITS name, for ITS sake, and without expectations of reward. Then you will see God in all ITS glory."

Doing just that, I had followed his advice and had indeed been taken from the human state to the top of the Mountain of God. But here, only a few hours later, I was again at the bottom of life, looking up. Why was the experience of God so short-lived?

My skin felt clammy. I felt weak, trembly, and sick to my stomach; my breath came in gasps. The image of Paul's face faded in and out of mind.

Then, a frightening presence entered the bedroom. It seemed like a hunched vulture at the foot of my bed, waiting with due patience for its reward. The specter was suddenly visible, and I knew him well. In ancient Greece he was called Thanatos; the old Romans knew him as Mors. It was none other than the Grim Reaper, the Angel of Death. A deputy to the Lords of Karma, he had come to escort me from the land of the living. He looked like a wizened old priest in a monk's habit. Nothing about him inspired fear, but neither was there any glimmer of love or compassion. His eyes shone like black marbles, and the network of fine, cross-hatched lines of his pale skin suggested old dairy cream in a jar that had gone sour. With my Spiritual Eye I could see him plainly, even though the room was dark and my head was beneath the covers.

The grim old man waited in silence. What was it that the ECK-Vidya had said through the bartender about what I would face tonight? But wait! When the time of death came, wasn't the Mahanta to take me to the other side? So what was this old man doing here?

The old monk beckoned for me to climb out of bed. Had he also waited in the shadows at the river? Even though my physical body lay huddled in bed, trying to get warm, I was in the Soul body. The Spiritual Eye made it possible to see from an overview where I was neither standing, sitting, nor lying down. It was an all-seeing position. Objects in my room had a living clarity, as if each article—dresser, picture, bedstead—were infused with a gently pulsating light. The shabby furnishings also looked clean and new. Literally, the only dark area surrounded the old monk. The space around him was devoid of lightness—leaden and somber. He beckoned a second time; I shook my head. He had missed his chance at the river and had come to try again.

Strangely, in the Soul body, I had no fear of him; at most, a mild curiosity. The old pictures of the Angel of Death as a skeleton dressed in a hooded cowl were overblown. And yet, I knew that he could appear in any guise he wished, to suit the image held by the person he had come to lead across the boundary of death. To the cruel and evil, he came as a specter of horror, because that appearance befitted their evil. To those of good character, he arrived in the company of loved ones who had gone on before.

A third time, the old monk beckoned me to follow. But the bond of karma that had once bound us to each other was gone: The Mahanta had freed me of it by the river. But through force of habit, the stubborn old monk refused to leave the room. He had been my guide in lifetimes past, and would be so now. In desperation, I called to the Mahanta for help.

"Please help, Paul!"

The atmosphere in my room suddenly changed from raw tension to one of warmth. The old man turned to leave, but stopped to mouth a warning with his lips: "Later." Then he melted into thin air. A moment later, I was back in my shivering human form. Although Paul's

151

love was evident, he did not appear. In the past, he had come in person, sometimes as a Blue Light. Where was he now?

Was the visit of the Angel of Death just a bad dream brought on by fever? If death really had been vanquished, might it not also be possible that I would be healed of this fever? But the chills went on.

The Angel of Death had gone, but restless thoughts, sliced in crazy patterns, took shape within my mind. It was not a fear of death that hung upon me now, but a deeper will to live. The experience of God had come but hours ago, during which life had pledged to break for me its seal of mysteries. Now was not the time to give up my will to live, but the life force was surely ebbing. Was the Angel of Death to collect upon his promise of "Later"? But who could help? Paul had just banished that grim old monk of death, whose hand was stayed a moment, yet some initiative now seemed to rest upon me. The Master was letting me handle the physical side of healing. It appeared unlikely that I would receive further aid from celestial sources, including Paul. His ousting of grim Death was past, a scene that now seemed as impossible as steam rising from an empty kettle.

In the kitchen next door, a cup clanged down upon a bare tabletop. Paper rustled against paper. Cathy, the landlady's teenage daughter, was turning the pages of what sounded like a magazine. The Golden-tongued Wisdom from earlier stole back into my awareness: I would go to a hospital tonight, but for me to survive, the hospital was to be one in another town. To survive. It meant that if I wanted to live, it was up to me to act. I wrestled myself from bed and knocked gently on the locked door to the landlady's kitchen.

"What is it?"

"I fell in the river. Would you call an ambulance?"

Medical aid was the next logical step to survival. My plan went no further than one step at a time. The ambulance would come, I would direct the medical crew to take me to a hospital in another city, and I would beat the Angel of Death a second time.

A moment of silence followed on the other side of the door, then came the rapid dialing of a phone number. In a muffled tone, Cathy spoke quickly to someone on the other end of the line. She dropped the receiver back on its cradle and called through the door, "They'll be here in a few minutes. Are you all right?" I assured her there was no immediate danger, and soon, the riffling sound of page-turning began again.

I wanted to live. The phone call had set events into motion; one thing would lead to another, and all I had to do was go along for the ride. People who were experts at handling emergencies would soon make everything OK. They would stop the shivering of my limbs which was beyond my control. Pneumonia was a real concern. What a trivial way to end this life—unloved and alone. Then I wondered, What clothes do you wear in an ambulance? I still had on my flannel pajamas, bathrobe, and winter coat. In spite of them, I froze. Maybe the ambulance would have better heat than this room.

About an hour after midnight, just as I was putting on a pair of slippers, the red light of an ambulance made eerie splashes of color upon my wall. No cars were driving on this residential street, so the ambulance had backed up over the curb, right up to my door. I pulled back the curtain in the front room to get a look. Neighbors were drifting out on their porches to see why the commotion. A rescue technician knocked on the door. I opened it and saw a stretcher set up on the sidewalk at the foot of the steps.

153

"You'll have to get on yourself," he said. "Otherwise we can't take you." This sounded like a strange directive. What if someone were unconscious? What if I had passed out in bed? Would a committee of rescuers have filed into my bedroom, then stood there helplessly while a spokesman explained, "We could have saved him, but he wouldn't get on the stretcher." At least part one of the plan was in motion: the ambulance had arrived. So I obliged him by lying down on the stretcher. Just that quickly, the medical technician and a helper strapped me to it. They were joined by the driver and his assistant, and the four men lifted me into the ambulance. My last glimpse of the neighbors was of frightened people; trouble had come too close.

"Where to?" asked the paramedic, who had come to the door.

When I named the hospital in the next town, he balked at the needless distance. "What's wrong with ours?" How was it possible to explain about the Golden-tongued Wisdom from the bartender? It was bad enough being carted around in the depth of night in an ambulance, without trying to win an esoteric discussion with a paramedic about something like that. But I persisted, so he leaned forward to talk with the driver. The conversation was out of hearing, because the ambulance was already moving fast, wailing its siren. Barring an accident enroute to the hospital, it seemed I had slipped from the sticky grasp of the old monk of death. I settled back for the ride.

Unexpectedly, my heart began to flutter in an odd way, flying against my ribs like a wild bird throwing itself against the bars of a cage. Then came dizziness and nausea. Perhaps the monk of death had fooled me. Maybe the paramedic was only humoring me about driving to the distant place. Maybe they felt that the

154

fever had made me delirious and would do what seemed best: drive to the closest hospital.

Far off, a train whistle broke the night. I tried to sit up on the stretcher, but the straps held me tight. "Which hospital are we going to?" I asked. "Stay put," the technician ordered.

"Where are we going?"

He shrugged and leaned forward to the driver for a second conference. The ambulance slowed at a street corner, then shot off in a new direction. Apparently, my suspicions had been right. With railroad tracks crossing the route to the local hospital, a long freight train could appear at this most importune time and block our way. The monk of death might then exert all his power to produce a crisis in my condition, and the net result would be his victory.

But the ambulance's change in direction from the near to the far hospital threw the monk's energies off-line, and so diffused them. Yet I was not out of trouble: my heart continued its irregular beating. Any minute, it seemed, I might leave this human body forever.

Again I called to Paul for help. Often, during my life in ECK, the sure presence of the Mahanta had brought comfort and aid in moments of despair. To perceive this treasured resource of spiritual aid demanded a full surrender of all worries. Such surrender is not for the proud. Self-will pushes the ego out front, but ego and love make poor bedfellows. And so, surrender means a love for the Mahanta more dear than one's own weakness.

But Paul gave no response. The monk of death I had seen, yet not a trace of the Mahanta, no matter how much I wanted to believe in his constant presence. The ambulance now raced through the dark, along a county road, and I felt alone. Forsaken by the Master?

The ride seemed to last an aeon. And I was certain that any delay—like a freight train blocking the tracks—would have caused my death. Yet, without any concrete evidence of Paul's presence, he seemed to have taken care of all arrangements for my good.

By the time the ambulance pulled up to the entrance of the emergency room, I was shaking uncontrollably from the waist down. The paramedics quickly carried me inside. A doctor came into the room to examine me on a cot, where they had placed me. He logged my temperature and pulse. "I'm going to keep you under observation for a while to see about that shivering." Then he pulled the curtain around my cot and stepped into the other room. Lights in the room were dimmed. I lay on my back, eyes on the ceiling, softly chanting HU, a pure name of God.

Then came the Blue Light, which announced the Mahanta. Paul *was* here. The Light was a dancing blue globe the size of a large pumpkin. It hung near the ceiling: at once near, yet as easily a massive star in outer space. The dimensions of the blue globe were actually uncertain, giving a feeling of both immediacy and tremendous distance all at once. With it came a warmth that reached to my bones, warming the chill of my wild shivering. My heart settled down and beat with more regularity. A few minutes later, this friendly light of love scattered and disappeared, but it left its love. I knew that Paul had been in the Light; indeed, he *was* the Light.

My body grew serene. A half hour later, the doctor drew the curtain aside for a follow-up exam. All readings appeared normal. He rechecked them several times, then said, "There's no reason to keep you any longer. The problem seems to be gone." He did not know that Paul had come as the Blue Light and given a spiritual healing.

156

I was not exactly dressed to catch a cab in my flannel pajamas, bathrobe, and winter coat, so the doctor called the police station for a patrol car. An officer arrived at the emergency room, and the doctor asked him to give me a lift home. In the squad car, I sat in silence, thinking of the Mahanta's perfect love. How could I have doubted his great love? Was it possible to even think that the Master would abandon one of his own in need?

One thing came of this: From this day on, I knew I could not live without the Master's love.

The night seemed to have reached an agreeable end. The Angel of Death had lost, but I sensed that the experience of God-Realization had just begun to transform my physical life. Little could I guess, however, that the ECK would again stir me to the core before the dawn. Or that tomorrow would see a departure from my old, but cozy, nest of convention.

We in ECKANKAR know that Jesus made a visit to the Katsupari Monastery.

18

Madness for God

"You ask me how I became a madman. It happened thus: One day, long before many gods were born, I woke from a deep sleep and found all my masks were stolen,—the seven masks I have fashioned and worn in seven lives,—I ran maskless through the crowded streets shouting, 'Thieves, thieves, the curséd thieves.'

"Men and women laughed at me and some ran to their houses in fear of me.

"And when I reached the market place, a youth standing on a house-top cried, 'He is a madman.' I looked up to behold him; the sun kissed my own naked face.... and my soul was inflamed with love for the sun, and I wanted my masks no more. And as if in a trance I cried, 'Blessed, blessed are the thieves who stole my masks.'

"Thus I became a madman."

—Kahlil Gibran
The Madman:
His Parables and Poems

159

* * *

In the allegory of the Last Judgment, recorded in Matthew 25:36, Christ is quoted as saying, "Naked, and ye clothed me: I was sick, and ye visited me: I was in prison, and ye came unto me."

Christian literature has no information about the life of Christ between his twelfth and thirtieth birthday, when his mission began. In the West, it is taken for granted that Christianity has the sole right to the history of Christ. But in central Asia, among people of the Islamic religion, it is known that Jesus spent his early years in Kashmir. They also have staked a claim on the person of Jesus: He—along with Adam, Noah, Abraham, Moses, and Muhammad—is a prophet of God. His travels took him all the way to northern India and Tibet.

Indeed, we in ECKANKAR know that Jesus made a visit to the Katsupari Monastery, where the ECK abbot in charge is Fubbi Quantz.

Mohammad Yasin, the author of *Mysteries of Kashmir,* contends that Jesus spent his silent years in Northern India and Tibet. And that after his crucifixion, which did not result in death, Jesus fled back to the region where he had spent the silent years. With him went Mary, his mother, who died on the journey and was buried in Murree, a town in Kashmir. Jesus, who was alternately known as Hazrat Isa and the prophet Yuz Asaf, then finished his mission, died, and was buried in Srinagar.

The reason for this background is not necessarily to endorse it, but to raise the question, What did Jesus do in the silent years from twelve to thirty? Should one pause to consider, Jesus likely did something with his life. Perhaps when he later gave his sermons, like the allegory about the Last Judgment—where he pictures himself as naked, sick, and imprisoned—he was draw-

160

ing upon actual experiences from his silent years. In other words, he did not lead a sheltered life. It is even possible that when the intoxication of God came upon him, he at the time may have acted very much like the individual described by Gibran in *The Madman.*

Critics will argue that this stretches a point. Yet mankind shows a flair for selecting a holy man as a model, then destroying the very spirituality he lived by reducing him to a myth. Therefore, Jesus the man, who was filled with the Holy Spirit and became the Christ, is made into a machinelike being who is without the traits of humanity: He does not marry; he sits life out for eighteen silent years; and yet, without experience as a human being, he is expected to minister wisely to people. It is a fantasy. Mankind in creating its gods makes them untouchable. There is no possible way to become like them, but only worship them. For this reason, mankind is rightly accused of creating God in its own preferred image. An image that conveniently ignores the smell of sweat or illness, and creates impossible standards of physical and spiritual perfection.

And yet a prophet of God is an exceptional being. He himself has walked in the shoes of mankind. He knows firsthand the suffering of the people he comes to serve. In spite of his suffering and his consequent understanding, he is made to endure untold indignities by the very ones he's come to give the Light and Sound of God.

He is a stranger, yet a kin. But in him there is a madness for God that is not understood by those around him; often not even by his closest disciples. And for that reason, he is an object of ridicule. Not until he is gone is his contribution to the spiritual upliftment of the human race grudgingly acknowledged. In time, the name of this agent of God is finally raised to social acceptance, even while the Godman of the modern age is mocked and rejected.

161

As I was buying my plane ticket, a heavy fog descended upon the airport, halting all arrivals and departures.

19

Off the Deep End

There is a reason the ECK Masters tell an aspirant to go slow in his efforts to see God. If thrust into ITS presence before the individual is conditioned spiritually, he will find it hard to integrate into his outer life the inner changes that have taken place. One who reaches the SUGMAD before he is ready may upend the codes of society and pay a price. In my case, the Mahanta was collapsing time. I had a long way to go in this lifetime to get ready for the spiritual leadership of ECKANKAR. The training of ECK Masters is thorough, far more rigid than anything one might find anywhere else. But the methods used are largely the secrets of the Vairagi Adepts.

The neighborhood had settled down by the time the police officer returned me to my lodgings. Porch lights were off, and houses were dark. Certain that the worst of the night was over, I climbed into bed, glad I had gotten off so easily.

Morning would come as usual, bringing with it the routines established during my short stay: clean up, walk to work, breakfast from a vending machine, and a long day of pushing a proofreader's pencil. But the longed-for routine was not to be; this became apparent when I tried to fall asleep. Somewhere in the house people were up talking, and this made it hard to sleep. Besides the nuisance caused by the low hum of voices, my mind now began its peculiar trick of speeding up. This had unnerved me as a child, and it unnerved me now. Like the flywheel on the corn sheller in our granary, it began slowly but surely to gain momentum. To keep from losing control of my mind, I was forced to hover on the edge of consciousness in order to monitor it.

My mind was like a runaway train. At normal speed it was a useful instrument, but when it raced out of control, every turn in the track brought the threat of disaster.

Struggling to govern this strange acceleration of my mental processes, I anxiously watched the window for a sign of dawn; then I could get busy and clean up for work. Perhaps activity would slow down my runaway mind. But the night hung on. Poor lighting made it impractical to read, and I had written letters to all my correspondents. No reason to seem pushy by writing a second letter before they answered the first.

The voices came closer. Pushing back the covers, I listened in the dark to determine who was holding a conversation. It sounded like two people talking in my room, but no one was there. The person now speaking was Cathy, who seemed to be chatting with a girlfriend. Their talk was about school things, just as it had been during their phone conversation a few hours ago. If nothing else, they kept me awake. But my speeding mind said, "Stand by!" Then I understood that the ECK-Vidya, the ancient science of prophecy, was about to speak. The ancient oracle was to foretell my future via the Golden-tongued Wisdom.

Sudden concern shadowed the voices of the two invisible girls. "Is he breathing?"

It seemed that an ethereal play was being presented for my benefit, to show what the morning might bring if I stayed in bed. Then I could see my room from the vantage point of Soul hovering near the ceiling. The room was lit by the daylight of midmorning. Beside my bed were the two teenagers; in it was my body, blue and apparently dead. Seeing that I had not gone to work as usual, Cathy had knocked on my door and gotten no response. Apparently, the girls had planned to cut classes that day, because Cathy's mother was in Arizona on vacation. Emboldened by her friend's company, Cathy had retrieved a key and opened the door between my room and the kitchen. This is the scene that the ECK-Vidya played out for me in the Soul body.

In this ethereal play, Cathy's friend gasped, "He's dead!"

Hearing this, despite the cold, I got out of bed and paced the floor. The Mahanta, through the ECK-Vidya, seemed to show me the scenario that would occur in the morning if I remained in bed. My racing mind would cause my heart to flutter, as my heart had done in the ambulance. That would be fatal.

Even though not six hours ago I had passed through the rite of God-Realization, and had then faced off against the Angel of Death, it seemed the old specter of mortality was ever there to haunt me. I wanted to live. The experience of God had impressed upon me what a great privilege life is, and my desire now was to live. Therefore, what the ECK-Vidya seemed to foreshadow was totally unacceptable. If the girls were to find me dead in bed, the solution was simple: get out of bed and stay out.

So I sat shivering in my chair, waiting the last few minutes before six o'clock, when I might clean up in the

165

bathroom without censure by the old-timers. As I sat there waiting, a stunning love for God swept through me. It stripped away the social order, revealing the power of love to make everything right. Indeed, everything was right. Clear as a light, I saw the superficiality of mankind's striving for wealth and honor. Position and fame were two meaningless smudges of dirt in the galaxies of God, where love ruled supreme.

Softly, I began to laugh. All my striving to fit into the self-serving molds of "What will people think?" suddenly hit me as silly and flighty. Did God care whether a person was Roman Catholic or Greek Orthodox, of the Missouri Synod or some other Lutheran church, a Jew or a follower of Islam? He knew what they were, just as he knew when a sparrow fell. But did he stop any of them from attending the church or temple of their choice, any more than he stopped the sparrow's fall? God simply knew all, loved all.

Thus did the power of divine love move my thoughts.

After cleaning up, I made a change in my usual routine. Instead of walking to the office, I decided to skip work. What better way to return God's love than to fly to Las Vegas and work for Paul? Unknown to me, he was on a trip to Europe. Like many unbalanced people before and after that day, I thought the Master would be waiting for me with open arms at the Las Vegas airport. Actually, an unbalanced person is a nuisance to himself and others. Paul didn't need someone like me in that condition.

It was a long walk to the bank, where I had a small savings account. By the time I arrived, the place had opened. I walked into the lobby and approached a teller, asking to close out my account. As she went about arranging the paperwork, a strong scent of roses permeated the lobby. The scent was overpowering. It gave the feeling that I was standing in a rose garden instead of the austere bank. But not a flower was to be seen anywhere.

When the teller finished counting out my money, I remarked, "The scent of roses must make this a pleasant place to work."

"There are no roses here," she said curtly.

Her comment puzzled me. Then an image flashed to mind of Paul. Somewhere in the ECK writings, he had told of fragrant aromas that were associated with certain ECK Masters. Even though the ECK Master might remain invisible, an individual could know the ECK Master was there by a pleasant, lingering floral scent. Then I suddenly understood that the scent of roses, which was sometimes linked with the saint Milarepa, today announced the presence of Paul, who was nearby in the invisible Soul form. My spirits lifted at the thought of it. This was all the more reason to fly to Las Vegas and offer my services to help him accomplish his mission.

Fired with zeal, I flagged a taxi. Before leaving my room for the bank, I had dressed in a suit a tailor had made for me in Japan. Servicemen who didn't waste their pay at downtown bars bought stereos and tailor-made suits and shirts, getting a head start on the right wardrobe for their careers in business after discharge from service.

"Where to?" asked the cabbie.

When I replied, "The airport," he said, "No bags?"

"No bags."

By now my divine mission to help Paul with ECKANKAR was becoming very clear. Of course, it really never dawned on me that I was very out of balance at that moment. All I could see in my imagination was Paul waiting for me at the Las Vegas airport. I must get there immediately.

The taxi driver was a philosopher. He mused about the dallyings of representatives in the halls of Congress, about the war in Vietnam, and about the changing face of religion in America. As he sermonized about national issues, I became still more out of balance. Now obsessed with the idea of surrender to the Mahanta, I wondered how best to demonstrate an emphatic rejection of the material world. Total surrender to the Master would be my final, highest gift of love. Unfortunately for the cabbie, he was about to become the object of my resolve to reach perfect surrender.

"That'll be $3.50," he said, as the cab stopped in front of the air terminal. I took out my wallet and shoved a fistful of dollars at him.

Taken aback, he shouted, "What's the matter with you? Give me my fáre and get out!"

Replacing the cash in my wallet, I tossed it on the seat between us. The combination of that and my glazed eyes were probably what made him reach for the door handle, ready to flee into the street. Then he slid the wallet across the seat at me like a hot puck, while bellowing, "Take your money and get out!"

It is no easy thing to surrender one's earthly goods to an angry cabbie. Anyway, the ride was free: The moment I got out he drove off, the tires of his taxi squealing loudly.

How did I expect to give away my money and yet buy a ticket to Las Vegas? A detail like that was of no concern: it could be dealt with later. In this odd frame of mind, I supposed I was living in the moment: a spiritual quality. Actually, it was a distortion of truth. Today, as I watch others demand the right to do as they please, it is plain how selfish their so-called acts of freedom really are. Actions done in the name of freedom but without regard for the rights of others are purely selfish. This was but one ugly potential I was to see in myself and others through this string of unfolding erratic deeds.

I went into the small terminal and bought a ticket. Now another strange coincidence occurred: a heavy fog descended upon the airport, halting all arrivals and departures.

The waiting room was full of commuters, most of whom were heading for Chicago. The heavy fog caused a second flight to cancel, then a third. People were continuing to arrive, and due to crowding, some were moving back outside.

While all this was going on, my judgment was becoming even more lopsided. I was beginning to enter a catatonic state, which was caused by the struggle of the spiritual and negative forces within me. The negative, or Kal, power was resisting the influence of ECK, which was slowly but surely making inroads into the physical from the high spiritual planes. This was causing a split in direction. The old me of habits and social convention was receiving the signals of ECK in a garbled manner, so that I might act rashly and fall under the permanent control of Kal. It was the Kal's last-ditch, all-out effort to keep me from spiritual freedom.

Later, when the passage of time allowed me to be more objective and put these experiences into perspective, I realized that so much of what people imagine about God-Realization is false. Even though the experience has an immediate effect upon Soul, it takes awhile longer for the transforming effects of God-Realization to work their way down through old emotions and mental patterns. The duration in which these changes take place is marked by chaos: The individual sees a complete turnabout in his life.

Martin Luther, as a student, had a revelation during a thunderstorm; he went on to become the great

Protestant reformer. Saul, on the road to Damascus, was blessed with the Light of God; he became Saint Paul, the foremost missionary of early Christianity. Moses, at the burning bush, had a spiritual vision; it transformed him from a lowly shepherd to the leader of the children of Israel.

Yet for all the known cases of individuals who had a divine revelation and became well-known characters in history, there are countless others who are unknown, and who lived much as they had in the past. With one difference: Their new outlook on life was a radical change from earlier.

Now, very much against my better judgment, I was convinced it was necessary to stand up in the waiting room and make a pronouncement. So I did. In a loud voice, I said, "Unless I say this, the fog cannot lift and more flights will be delayed." Then I sat down. Horrified at what I had done, I looked neither left nor right. Yet the people straight ahead, in my direct line of vision, gave a fair indication of what the rest were doing around me. They were throwing frightened glances my way. By now, everyone was more anxious than ever to vacate the waiting room and get on board.

Then, just as I had predicted, the sun broke through the clouds and the agent at the desk made an announcement over the PA system: "There has been an unexpected break in the cloud cover. The plane for Chicago will now board. Please have your boarding passes ready."

Even though my body was sinking into a rigid state, like a trance, I was fully aware of everything going on around me. When the ticket agent had announced that the flight to Chicago was ready to board, a rental-car agent at a desk in the waiting room shouted encouragement at me, "Hey, buddy! You got it right on!"

Unfortunately, the flight that was boarding was an earlier flight number, and I was required to take my seat again, along with a lot of other disappointed passengers.

My pronouncement had embarrassed me greatly. I wanted only to get on board and hide in my seat. The sooner the plane arrived in Chicago, the sooner I would be away from all these people who had seen me acting like a fool. But there was more to come.

Just as quickly as the first plane took off, the fog closed in heavier than ever. The ticket agent announced that the next flight, which was mine, would board as soon as the fog broke again. I sat passively in my seat. Even though the place was crowded, the seats to my immediate left and right were understandably vacant. All the while, I was trying to have a discreet inner conversation with Paul. The more I thought about him, the more it seemed he was no longer in Las Vegas, but much closer—in Chicago. It was therefore imperative for me to get there soon. But still I sat like a mummy, hoping against hope that nothing would draw me into a bigger mess than I was already in.

The second time the urge came to speak, I delivered a mishmash of my perceptions of truth. Mercifully, this address was brief. When I finished and sat down like a robot, several more seats emptied on either side of me.

During this awful morning at the airport, I learned a lot about people who cross over to the far side of what society considers proper behavior. These unfortunate ones are so caught up in their world of delusion that they often display no sense of social conscience. As Gibran said in *The Madman,* "I woke from a deep sleep and found all my masks were stolen." The masks of illusion. The masks which the majority of people wear seven deep, but are unconscious of wearing. Haughty

171

people devoid of either compassion or insight who mock the deranged, smugly certain they would never stoop to such behavior. Moreover, they are unable to recognize one who has been touched by the grace of God.

Following my second announcement, I actually prayed for the fog to lift and let me go. But the ECK was in control of things. I was too out of balance at that time to be of help to Paul. In fact, it was hardly safe for me to venture out in public. Therefore, the Mahanta was going to salvage a very negative experience and turn it into a useful one.

Meanwhile, my disjointed thoughts ran like this: All I have must be surrendered to God.

How many times has it been said in the ECK writings that this surrender relates only to the inner self? The Master does not want an initiate's possessions. Nor is a person asked to give up his family or job. All that is asked of him is to surrender his attachment to material things. He may then find enjoyment in the things provided for this life; but should they be lost due to misfortune, he will pick himself up and show gratitude for what blessings he retains. That is the meaning of *surrender* in ECKANKAR.

This was something I had yet to learn, despite the previous night on the bridge.

Many things happen in threes, because three elements are needed to finish a creative cycle. Waiting for the next flight to board, I pondered what else I might do to achieve complete surrender. Then the thought came to disrobe. Sick at heart, I nonetheless got up to follow out the latest instructions. As I removed my coat and tie and began to unbutton my shirt, a big man barked, "Hey, Mac, you can't do that! Call the cops."

My inner voice, acting like a transmitter for the Kal, said, "Turn to the entrance. Paul is here."

Paul here?

Slowly I turned, and waited. And waited. By now I was immobile, standing like a pillar of salt. As I faced the door, I saw auras appear around people as they entered the building. Each aura was a soft white, differing from another only in how far it reached out from each individual. The brightness of an aura reflected the spiritual unfoldment of that person. And everyone had an aura.

My expectations grew higher. "Any minute now," said the inner voice of Kal, "Paul will come for you." The door opened and two men in blue uniforms walked in. With them was a man in a cheap suit, who seemed to be in charge.

"You'd better come with us," he said.

He took me by the arm, and I followed him out the door to a police car. An officer opened the back door, put his hand on top of my head to prevent me from banging it on the top of the door, then sat me down inside. All the while I maintained my trancelike silence. The two men in blue climbed into the front seat, while the plainclothesman was stuck in back with me. The car lurched forward, and I knew we weren't going to meet Paul.

I had fallen as far as I could fall. Anything I ever cared about was left behind, refuse from a past life that had ended the night before on the bridge. Few in the clergy would understand that love is what brought me here. Love for God is what had shattered the outer structure of my social acceptability. No matter if I had been tricked by the negative force, I was responsible for my own actions. No matter what happened in the next few minutes, I still loved the Mahanta. Alternately I flew between the extremes of love and fear, wondering what would become of me now.

The driver was in no hurry to reach his destination; he drove at a leisurely pace. Dropping the trance, I said to the detective, "I can speak now." He ignored my remark completely. He hardly responded, as if a fly hitchhiking on the outside of the car window had addressed him.

Nothing to do but sit and wait.

A gentle wind, like the Wind of ECK, suddenly entered the room as the heavy metal and wooden door swung open on its hinges.

20

I Am Always with You

A common misunderstanding in ECK is that unless one specifically asks for the Mahanta's presence, the Master is off someplace else. Fortunately, this is not true. In the Soul body, the Mahanta is all-knowing, all-powerful, and able to be in all places at once.

When a problem arises that outpaces an ECK initiate's ability to handle alone, he is driven to look outside himself for aid. By placing his attention upon the Mahanta, he calls forth the miraculous power of ECK: then all things are possible. And in that moment of awakening, he realizes that the Master has been with him all along. There never was a barrier of separation to keep them apart, except for the blindness of the seeker. The Master reveals his presence by some means, and now the ECK is on the field. The initiate, although mindful that he must undergo whatever ordeal he has asked deliverance from, can now play the role of spectator as well as actor. He is an observer in the audience, watching a scene from his life unfold. At the same time, he is the leading character.

Spiritually, he stands at the peak of awareness. In this high state of expectancy, he absorbs the lessons

177

needed to avoid a replay of this scene ever again. And life goes on.

* * *

The police car pulled into a parking lot beside a brick fortress. The driver stopped near a heavy metal door, and the detective waited while the two officers in front got out. Then he opened his door, while a policeman opened mine.

My appearance was unkempt by now. The tailor-made suit coat I carried over my arm. My shirt was open at the top; the tails of my shirt were out. Dangling from a coat pocket was my tie, where I had stuffed it to keep it from getting lost.

The plainclothesman led the way inside past the metal door. A narrow hallway led to a tiny lobby with two elevator doors that opened only with keys. The place seemed to have high security. A door swished open, revealing an elevator; my escorts prodded me to step inside. Upstairs in a dark chamber was a high desk at which sat a sergeant.

He turned his hard eyes upon me. "Stuff in that shirt!"

I was back on earth; all spaciness gone. And so was the delusion that Paul was just around the corner, holding back just a moment longer to see how I might react to just one more test before he would appear and deliver me from this embarrassment. No longer did I expect Paul, in his physical body, to come into the room and order, "Release him, sergeant; he's with me." I was on my own. It seemed that Paul did not, could not, exist in this harsh world: jail. A place for criminals, but certainly not for me.

The sergeant asked the detective a few questions and wrote the responses in a ledger, as far as I could tell from my position at the foot of the high desk.

Two new men joined our intimate circle. They also wore blue uniforms, but, unlike the police officers who had brought me in, they did not wear guns. "Come along," said one. The detective breathed a sigh; his part was done.

This time we rode the elevator up higher. When it stopped, we entered a floor with white walls and bars. One man led the way, unlocking barred doors; the other brought up the rear. The metal doors clanged shut in a perfectly final way as we passed through them. Powerless to do anything but ride the current of events, I began to wonder if an attitude of acceptance, such as I now had, was the true meaning of surrender. There was no fear, no hope—only moment-to-moment existence. This social machinery was too concrete for me to resist, to bluff, to outwit, to do anything with but accept.

Our walk halted at the very end of a long corridor, which was bordered on the right by barred windows overlooking a tree-lined street; on the left, by rows of cells.

As our party stopped in front of what was to be my cell, a bearded man with wild hair in the next cell called to the jailers, "Hey, when do I get out of here?"

"You can rot, buddy!"

"Hey, tough man! What you got against me?"

The barred door slammed shut behind me. The measured footsteps of the jailers echoed hollowly down the corridor. Another clanging of heavy metal as the outside door rolled shut. Then silence.

"What are you in for?" asked the wild-looking man from the other side of the chipped-and-scarred wall between us that had once been painted a uniform, flat white.

"Disturbing the peace."

179

He gave his name as if he were a celebrity and I should know him. "You read the papers about me?"

"I haven't read any papers," I said.

"TV?" he asked hopefully.

"Don't have one," I replied, suddenly very tired.

After a pause, he exclaimed with pride, "They caught me selling pot."

He prattled on while I surveyed my new surroundings. Like it or not, this was home; I felt lost, like a puppy in a pet shop.

This was a short-term facility. The double bunk, top and bottom, had soiled mattresses, but no sheets or blankets. A water bubbler was in the corner beside a toilet bowl, the wooden seat removed. On the filthy concrete floor was a soiled roll of toilet paper. No place had been provided to hang clothes, so I used the bedpost for my suit coat. After standing up as long as possible to avoid touching the dirty mattress, I was finally left no choice but to stand there indefinitely or to lie down on it.

Some fine mess I'd gotten myself into. Yet every time I shut my eyes, the clear white Light of God filled my inner vision, restoring the contentment that fled so easily in this alien place. The lack of sleep the night before had left me weary, and so I slept.

Sometime later, it seemed as if a set of steel wheels were bouncing over a nearby cobblestone walk. Was the noise from someone pulling the sharpened disks of a harrow along the gravel in our driveway on the farm? Until opening my eyes, I thought for a second that I might be home on the farm in my old bed; but such was hardly the case. It was the steel gate at the end of the corridor rumbling open. I reawakened to the very nightmare from which sleep had so kindly whisked me away.

"Here's lunch," said the jailer brusquely. He shoved a plastic tray through an opening at the bottom of my door, then retreated.

The prisoner in the next cell bartered for my dessert, a flat piece of brown cake. The only eating utensil on the tray was a spoon. The officials did not entrust prisoners with sharp objects like knives. The mashed potatoes were cold and hard, the gravy on top like a watery glue. The vegetables were overcooked, therefore soggy, and also cold. Eating what little I could, I pushed the tray back out through the opening.

As I faced the door of the cell, I could see through the bars that lined the windows on the other side of the walkway. All that was visible from my cell were the bare tops of trees. The sounds of traffic in the street below raised in me a desperate feeling of claustrophobia, like a caged animal might feel. But there was nothing to do about it. So I lay down on the bunk again and tried to blank out my wretched environs. Alternately I drifted between sleep and wakefulness, and the sharp divisions of time melted into a soft wave where it was hard to tell one from the other.

The hours passed as I floated in and out of the body. On the inner planes were always the Sound and Light. When the jailer brought supper, I ignored it for the serene bliss of the more kindly inner worlds. When he returned for the tray, he asked, "Hey, don't you want any?" I mumbled no and drifted away from earth again.

It was a wonderful state to be in, this nonstate of physical consciousness. This experience of landing in jail had cleared up one thing for me: When Paul said, "I am always with you," he was speaking as the Inner, not the Outer, Master. It was Paul as the Mahanta, not as the Living ECK Master of the physical body. Such an insight might appear simplistic today, but it was not to

181

me then. ECKANKAR was new. So many ideas that Paul brought out rested upon principles from the Far East, where such phenomena as Masters mysteriously appearing out of thin air were still accorded a ready acceptance.

The Far East was not yet made indifferent to such things by advances in scientific thinking, as was the West. There, and in ECKANKAR, all things were possible. Faith still had power. Who was to say that Spirit might not suspend the rigid laws of matter to satisfy Its own aims?

After all, did not Jesus say in old-time Christianity: "If ye have faith as a grain of mustard seed, ye shall say unto this mountain, Remove hence to yonder place; and it shall remove; and nothing shall be impossible unto you"?

That night my sleep was continually touched by the musical sounds of the Holy Spirit. Sometimes there came the elegant tinkling of celestial bells that had no counterpart on earth. At other times I heard the jubilant songs of birds, even though it was after midnight and the city had otherwise grown still. Oh, sweet music of God! Because of my love for God, and my clumsy, inappropriate way of expressing it among his other children, I was in jail. For a moment, the irony of it brought a wry smile of amusement to my lips, but the hard fact of my surroundings quickly muffled such levity.

Well after sunup, a cold mush, which was supposed to be milk and cereal, appeared through the hole in the cell door. One look at it chased my appetite. So I returned to my shabby mattress, unshaven and sorely in need of a shower. When the door on trolley wheels rolled open again, I expected it would be the jailer come to retrieve the breakfast tray. But this time there were two men. One unlocked my door and said, "Get your coat; you've got company."

Now I understand why prisoners leave their cells every chance they get: to break the monotony. Nearly any change is welcome for the little freedom it may bring.

The guards led me out of the cellblock. The clanging doors parted, leaving me respectful of their mechanical voice. Once shut, they might never reopen. We walked through several corridors, the guards flanking me in the event I tried to run for it. But it would have been ridiculously easy to catch me. Once the alarm sounded, and the outside door locks were snapped shut automatically, all they had to do was scout around inside for someone with a day's growth of beard and rumpled clothing. Maybe it's one reason prisoners were not permitted to clean up while in custody: An escapee would be easy to spot among the civilians.

The traffic in the corridors thinned as we reached a remote corner of the floor. The guards led me to a room where a solid wooden door, with bars bolted to the inside, barricaded the single entrance. In the room was a conference table.

"Take a seat," ordered the guard with the keys.

The mighty door with a peephole slammed shut, and I was alone. The windows were open, but bars on the outside discouraged any hope of flight. It looked like a beautiful spring day, but there was not the slightest chance I would get to enjoy it. And while I waited by the table, my thoughts returned to Paul, the Mahanta.

Where was he? Now I knew the difference between the Outer and Inner Master. No, Paul would not come through that heavy door at the end of the room. Whatever happened today, it was all up to me. And perhaps not even up to me: I forgot for a moment that this was jail. No use in looking to Paul for help in here. To do that would prove me a complete fool. Why should Spirit bend

Its laws to let me off the hook? I had offended society, and it demanded repayment. So I would pay. The heavy door was not going to spring open by itself. Better to accept my lot and take the punishment that was coming to me.

Then came the metallic sound of a key working the lock, and the heavy barred door swung open. Two young men entered the room in a lively, businesslike manner. Quickly sizing me up and determining I was harmless, the one with straw-colored hair said to the guards, "We'll be all right. Wait outside until I call."

The guards stepped from the room, and the imposing door clunked shut after them. A key rattled the lock, and a hand tested the doorknob for security.

The two young men introduced themselves as the assistant district attorney and a social worker. They had come to lay out my options. I asked about the money in my wallet, which was taken the night before when I was booked, hoping to use it for bail. The assistant DA shook his head. "You may need professional help. It won't do you any good to go back out on the street. If you post bail, you will be charged with disturbing the peace. It's not a serious offense, but you should take this opportunity to get professional help if it's needed."

What this came down to was that I was to commit myself to a hospital for an indefinite stay, to undergo a psychological evaluation. This would permit the authorities to make an examination at their leisure to decide whether there was really anything wrong with me. What was the best course of action? The two men sat across the table, waiting for my decision, while I reclined in my chair — my thoughts upon Paul. Of myself, I felt inadequate to decide an issue that would certainly alter my future. Should I dog it out: ignore the advice of these counselors and accept the civil punishment? Or would it be wiser to commit myself to a hospital for observation?

As I sat at the table, looking out the window at the tops of trees which were beginning to show little buds, I spoke inwardly to the Mahanta: Are you still with me, Paul?

A gentle wind, like the Wind of ECK, suddenly entered the room. And as it did, the heavy metal and wooden door swung open on its hinges. The two young men spun around in their chairs as the guards outside rushed to fill the doorway. Everyone was baffled. The door had been carefully locked; no one had touched it. Yet it had unlocked itself and swung open as though by invisible hands. The guards checked the workings of the lock, and the one with the keys said, "The lock's OK. I don't know what happened." They relocked the door and took up their former positions outside the room, but with less certainty than before.

But I had my answer. The locked door that apparently opened by itself was the Mahanta speaking through the ECK-Vidya. He said that the two young men were offering me an open door out of my trouble.

Without further ado, I said, "Let's do it your way."

The guards let them out, then returned me to my cell until the young men could make arrangements with the court for my transfer to the county hospital. As we approached my cell, I knew the hand of ECK was at work to help me out of this predicament, yet it would take time. This decision would launch me into vastly different circumstances.

Waiting on the edge of the bunk, I wondered what was in my cards.

I could no longer glibly say what ECKANKAR was, so Don had to be satisfied with the offer of a book.

21

Spirits of a Different Kind

Science has raised the standard of living beyond anything our grandparents might have imagined. Infant mortality is down, treatment for serious diseases is progressing nicely, fewer cavities for our children, better nutrition, and we and our offspring have the promise of a longer life expectancy. Yet for all its strides in health—physical, emotional, and mental—science is the first to admit that it is engaged in a never-ending war against the march of mortality.

But what is missing from science—in spite of its growing expertise in treating a weakness of the body, emotions, or mind—is a grasp of those forces from the inner worlds that use human frailty as a passport into the consciousness of some unfortunate people. I'm speaking of possession by evil spirits. Possession is not a biological phenomenon—even though a genetic defect may allow an astral entity the opening to attach itself like a parasite to a victim.

Not only can evil spirits join themselves to a person, they can also jump from him to another who gets overly sympathetic about the plight of the possessed individual. Spirits can hop around, even as fleas transfer from the lawn to a pet. But there is a way to guard against such invasion. When around a victim of possession, one can put his thoughts upon the Mahanta. Nor dare he let his emotions run amuck over that person's condition. ECKists who are doctors or nurses have learned in medical school how to be at once detached yet sensitive about their patients. They will not usually be troubled by entities if they keep their attention upon the Mahanta.

But a psychiatrist, a healer of science who deals with mental, emotional, and behavioral disorders, runs a greater-than-average risk of picking up a transient evil spirit from a patient. The field of medicine is said to have the highest rate of suicide among all occupations. Ironically, however, the highest incidence of suicide within the medical circle is among psychiatrists. Science, for all its miracles of juggling biology, cannot yet defend itself from the astral entities who cause the suicides. The scientific method itself may be at fault. Its research is restricted to physical evidence that must not only be observable, but also repeatable. The problem that science encounters here is that astral phenomena do not follow the laws of the physical world.

However, science is not completely helpless. When astral entities ride down into a victim through a weakness in his genetic structure, science can often control them by fortifying his inner defenses through the administration of drugs. This brings relief.

In ECK, we know that evil spirits can indeed possess people. Using one victim as a home base, they may transfer to a second or third person: possession allows them to enjoy secondhand experiences from the physical plane. Entities select their victims from among those with: (1) a genetic weakness (a past-life karmic condition); (2) a lack of self-discipline, such as in alcoholism (either present- or past-life karma); or (3) a strong empathy for a victim of possession (a combination of present- and past-life karma).

The fact of possession by evil spirits is also taken for granted in the Christian Bible. On one occasion, Jesus confronted a group of devils who had invaded the inner states of two people, whose home was in tombs near the roadside. So fierce were they that travelers were afraid to pass by the tombs. When the evil spirits realized that Jesus was going to cast them out, they begged him for permission to possess a herd of swine in the distance. Jesus agreed. Immediately, "the whole herd of swine ran violently down a steep place into the sea, and perished in the waters." That did nothing to endear Jesus to their owners.

Possession is but one of a thousand afflictions to beleaguer the human race. All such conditions spur on the purification of Soul. In whatever form an illness may appear, it is a perfect occasion for an individual—and his family, friends, and doctors—to become more aware of what one's responsibility is to himself and others.

* * *

One of my brushes with astral entities came about in this way.

After meeting the assistant DA and the social worker, I was again taken to my cell by guards. Then, right before noon, the gate at the end of the corridor rumbled open to proclaim their return. Two men in blue led me into the rather bleak chamber of a courtroom, where the assistant DA and the social worker were busy reviewing documents at a table. Greeting me, they informed me we were next on the docket. Once more they reminded me of the plan to admit myself to the county hospital for observation.

Without the benefit of a shave or shower, I wondered whether the judge might be influenced by an untidy appearance to dole out a harsher sentence. The bailiff called my name.

"Step to the line," he said.

Painted on the floor, several yards from the judge's bench, was a red line. The judge in his black robe was an imposing figure: he seemed a stern but fair man.

First, he read the people's complaint against me for disturbing the peace. Next, he read into the record advice from the assistant DA that I admit myself to the county hospital for observation. Recalling Paul's stirring assurance earlier that day in the consultation room, I was willing to take a chance on the hospital as my open door to freedom: the best way to rebalance the disorder my actions had caused. So I accepted the court's direction.

Within the hour, the social worker and I were on the road to retrieve my clothing from my room. When we pulled up outside the landlady's house, Don, the social worker, said, "Just tell her you're leaving. Pay up your rent, pack, and let's go." Fortunately, the rent was paid up. Our karmic score was settled.

In my room one last time, I was able to get a more objective look at its gloomy condition. Meeting the stranger on the bridge had changed things: at least in respect to my room and job. Had we not met, life today would be predictable—the way I preferred it. Right now I'd be in the proofroom, reading a galley on paleontology, a medical review, or copy for a math textbook that dripped with formulas, superscripts, and subscripts. No matter how dreary or uninspiring the job might have appeared to someone else, it suited me well. Who would ever have thought that a company would actually pay me for the privilege of reading? But it now looked as though my career in publishing was over.

While Don watched, I began to pack my few things in a suitcase. Curious about my collection of ECK books and discourses, he asked, "What is ECKANKAR?"

Who was I to say? Whatever definitions of it had once so glibly come to mind now seemed foolish in light of the experience on the bridge. What was ECK—Soul Travel? Love? Who could say? Rather than benefiting from a concise verbal description, Don had to be satisfied with the offer of a book: *ECKANKAR—The Key to Secret Worlds*.

As special as the ECK books were to me, the discourses were far more precious. I sensed that the hospital staff would sift through my reading material in order to create a profile of my condition. The ECK discourses are secret teachings. How far did my responsibility extend toward safeguarding them? As Don flipped through the book, I said, "Here's an armful of ECK books. Have all you want." Had I been secretive and held out on him, he would have seized whatever material—like the ECK discourses— seemed of value to me.

"One's enough," he said. "I just wanted an idea of what it was."

While Don was preoccupied with the book, I stashed all my ECK discourses and dream journals into the bottom of a grocery sack, covering them with trash. Unknowingly, Don helped carry my priceless treasures to the garbage can outside the house. I was now ready to face whatever lay ahead.

After Don helped me with admission into the hospital, many events during the three weeks of my stay became a mishmash. Every day was like the last, a peculiar world where the usual framework of time and space was hung in suspension.

191

Something odd happened during my first night in the hospital which might really have changed my life for good. The admission process had left me in a daze. After Don left, an attendant led me to a room where my personal belongings were inventoried and put into storage. What was I to wear? I found out soon enough. Our next stop was a clothing room in the basement that had the cluttered look of a welfare shop. Clothes there were donations for patients in long-term care. My attendant and the room's supervisor picked through a stack of used articles and chose for me a gruesome brown shirt and a baggy pair of clashing green pants. This was my outfit. The mismatched colors nearly made me retch.

After changing clothes, I was dismayed to see my tailor-made suit, white shirt, and good tie being jammed into a brown paper bag. The attendant handed the bag to a staff worker to take to the inventory room, where it would be added to my other things.

By now it was after serving hours for supper. My attendant took me to a corner table in the cafeteria and brought out bread and a bowl of soup. I wasn't hungry for much more. My attendant was a burly man of few words. He did not seem to expect much in the way of intelligence from those whom he served. He led me into a ward with patients who threw me strange looks. I was taken aback by a little man standing in a corner, wailing and cursing at invisible beings. Later, I learned he was possessed by spirits. From all appearances, he gave them a hard time.

My curiosity was aroused. What kind of a ward was this? My attendant had me sign in at the nurses' station where a nurse said, "Twenty minutes till lights out. You may walk anywhere in this ward, but the outside doors are locked."

After digesting that bit of news, I decided to stroll through the halls to see what the place had to offer. A door burst open and three men in white uniforms came into the ward with a struggling man who cursed even more viciously than the little man in the corner. By now my eyes were rolling at the unusual things going on around me. At the end of one corridor was a game room with a pool table. Oh nice, I thought, something to do. As I picked up the pool cue, a young man with a wan smile and vacant grey eyes came over to watch.

"Let me play!" he demanded.

Who's to argue? I thought, surrendering the cue.

He took a shot at a ball near the side pocket, missed, then caught the escaping ball with his hand and dropped it neatly into a pocket. "Your shot," he said. I lined up carefully for a long shot at the far end of the table. The young man, seeing me aim, walked to the pocket where I hoped to sink the ball, then blocked the pocket as I shot.

"Hey," I protested, "what's the deal?"

"You missed," he replied. "It's my turn." It seemed I had plenty to learn about the house rules.

That ended my interest in pool, so I headed toward the nurses' station. The idea of spending the night here was giving me the jitters. A male attendant showed me to the shower room, handed me soap and a towel, then disappeared. Luckily no one else was in the shower. It had been a full day, leaving me wary of further surprises.

After my shower, the attendant returned. "Come this way to your room," he said, as if to a vegetable. I traipsed meekly along to an austere room of white walls, white sheets, white wall lamp, and white closet. Only the floor was grey. The hospital bed much resembled an Air Force cot, except it stood higher: with handles at the end to crank the mattress up and down. The oak door had a square window in it, which gave the ominous feeling of being under observation; which, it occurred to me, I was.

In the closet were pajamas, a bathrobe, and shower clogs. I changed clothes, then went out into the hall to look around for five minutes until bedtime at ten. The door next to my room stood open. Inside, an old man lay on his bed, with a bottle of oxygen on a table beside him. He was asleep. Suddenly, as I was about to walk on, he gave a great shout. The shout receded into a plea, a sort of whimper: he begged to be left alone. But he was alone. The raspy sound of labored breathing accompanied his pleading. He began to thrash on the bed, but no one heard him. The man, who seemed on the verge of death, appeared to be in a final contest with unseen combatants.

I ran to the nurses' station for help. A nurse followed me to my neighbor's room, took one look, then raced off for reinforcements. A doctor hurried into the room, followed by several people in white uniforms. The nurse whom I had summoned stood with me outside in the hall. Her face, the color of chalk, was riveted upon the scene in the room, where attendants struggled to hold the old man down for the doctor.

Always willing to help in a crisis, I said to her, "If I can do anything to help, please let me know." But she acted as if I were even more ghostly than the invisible assailants of the old man. The realization finally sank in: She thinks I'm like the old man!

As Soul, I rested serenely inside my head, looking out at this bewildering corner of hell. I knew I had my wits about me and was all right; but what of the others? Were they OK? In my short stay of a few hours, I had seen suggestions of brutality from the hospital staff, as the three orderlies had brought that patient into the ward with more force than the occasion seemed to demand. That was a kind of madness, too. But it had the sanction of authority. My position here, I decided, was a precarious one. The patients were from a hostile world, but so was the medical staff that was in charge of treatment. I was to develop stronger opinions on the subject later.

The old man's breathing was a horrible thing to hear. It seemed every breath might be his last. Nevertheless, he hung on into the night; I could hear medical personnel stirring in his room until about 4:00 a.m., when everything suddenly became still. Later, I learned it was the hour of his death; before that time arrived, however, I would meet the entities who possessed him.

After the nurse failed to acknowledge me, I decided it was time to retire to my room for the night. It was satisfying to see that this bed was many times cleaner than the one in jail. But it was so high off the stone floor that my feet dangled when I sat on the mattress, making me wonder how long I could maintain this perch in my sleep without landing on the floor.

The room was quiet, but too bright. Light poured in through the square window in the door; otherwise, the room was barren of windows. Let's make the best of this, I thought, guardedly pleased with the improvement in my accommodations over the previous night. Sleep was hard to come by. Every few minutes a fresh murmur of voices rose next door. I wondered how the old man was getting on. Every half hour, a shadow darkened the little window in my door as an observer pressed his face to the glass to check on me.

About 2:00 a.m., I finally drifted into a troubled sleep. The air in the room seemed electric. I did not know it then, but the electricity was caused by three evil spirits who had taken up residence in the man next door, and who now had come to visit me. For years they had lodged inside him, destroying any chance he might have had for a normal life. But tonight the man was to die: This meant their eviction from that dwelling. It was high time to shop for new living quarters.

I awoke in my Astral body. The room looked pretty much the same as the physical one, except that three men of ghoulish appearance kicked open the door of my room and burst in. Then I knew: They had plans to possess me before the night was over. Two of the entities came at me from the front, the third edged around to the side of the bed, hoping to attack from behind. Still in the parallel astral world, I jumped out of bed and got into a crouch. The two psychic criminals rushed at me, but I stepped to the side. Then began a vicious thumb-jamming, eye-gouging, hair-pulling fight for my life that I could never have imagined in my wildest dreams. Again and again, they attacked. Each time I repelled them.

The savage attack taught me an important lesson about entities. They invade one's Astral body the way physical thugs would roll a street victim.

All this time I was chanting HU and calling upon Paul for help, but the outcome depended largely upon my own efforts. The Mahanta would give only as much support as I had developed through the Spiritual Exercises of ECK. Too many in ECK are lazy about developing their spiritual side. They do not take the ECK program seriously. If trouble comes, they just call on the Mahanta to fix things. Then, when things go sour, they chastize the Mahanta for deserting them. Actually, they have deserted him. They must understand that he offers each person the spiritual defenses needed to overcome any obstacle. It is their choice, however, to use whatever self-discipline is needed to take advantage of his help. After all, pain is usually the catalyst that starts people on the road home to God.

ECK is not a social welfare system. The Mahanta does, however, outline a way for each individual to surmount the trials of life and evolve into a greater spiritual being.

The three entities came at me repeatedly. My strength was beginning to fail, but so was theirs. One last fierce onslaught from me sent them into retreat. Two of the evil spirits staggered out of the door, while the third crawled, helped by my foot.

I awoke drenched in sweat. A man's eyes came to the window as I pretended to lie there asleep. The experience had been frightening, but victory had also given me a sense of self-worth. At no time in religious school had I been taught the ways and means entities might use to possess a victim. I had a new respect for these creatures of the lower Astral Plane. They were nothing to fool around with, anymore than a person would go into a rough part of town alone at night. But I had no choice in the matter. The judge had not warned me about possession when he offered me choices the day before. Neither he nor the assistant district attorney nor the social worker had any idea what kind of a hell they were suggesting for my health. They just did not know.

About four in the morning, the time later given to me as the hour the old man died, I again awoke in the Astral body. The door handle to the room was slowly turning. Springing out of bed again, I met the rush of the two entities who had earlier attacked from the front. Their friend apparently was in no shape to help in this battle. The fight was vicious, as had been the first, but my assailants were not nearly so strong as before. This struggle lasted only minutes. I threw them out of the room without ceremony. Where they went next is anyone's guess. Returning to the physical body, I rubbed my eyes, half expecting the assailants to appear in physical bodies and go for round three.

Punctual as ever, the observer's eyes looked in the window. I continued to chant HU, because it is a song of love to God. Right then I needed love.

As ever, dawn was a welcome friend bearing a gift of warmth and light. After its arrival, I was able to catch a few winks of sorely needed rest.

By now, I naturally began to wonder at each daybreak: What has the Mahanta in store for me today? There was a lot to learn about my surroundings, but I hoped to avoid further encounters with evil spirits looking for a home.

By letting me do as I pleased, they could snatch away
any products of my imagination for study.

22

What Happened in the Library

That first night in the hospital was memorable for what it taught about forces of the inner worlds that could shatter people's lives. The experience of astral entities who tried to possess me had surely been one of terror, but spiritual training by the Mahanta had allowed me to ward them off.

I would have liked to talk with someone about the experience, as a child might share a nightmare with a parent, but ironically, the hospital was hardly the time or place. What purpose would it serve to call the doctors' attention to more problems they would likely not understand anyway? Weren't there already enough? So I chose to play the game and be a star patient: maintain a low profile and keep my spirits up no matter what came in the way of treatment. Soon the doctors would release me, seeing that I posed no threat to the established order. That was my plan to regain freedom. By playing the game, I hoped to beat it.

But the Mahanta would teach me the futility of trying to twist the Law of Cause and Effect to my advantage. There still remained the unfinished business of disturbing the peace: the reason for my admission into the hospital. The Mahanta would demonstrate that no one ever climbs so high spiritually that he can brush aside a fair law. And how would Paul tutor me in this principle of cause and effect? By appearing in the Soul body for a heart-to-heart talk? That was unlikely, since it provided too easy a way out. No, I would have to go the full route of detainment, even though it was of my own volition.

Through long experience, the ECK Masters know people are headstrong about the laws of Spirit. The Masters may spell out an ECK principle a hundred different ways, yet people try to outdo each other in ongoing attempts to outsmart it. Why? Simply because they honestly think it's possible to get something for nothing. They cannot believe that their present burdens are hooked up with old, forgotten misdeeds from the past.

Certainly, my own problem was barely lukewarm before I had concocted a plan to speed my departure from the hospital: to play the game. Before my parting, however, I would learn unflattering things about myself and others. Perhaps the greatest discovery of all concerned the slender margin that separates the sane from those of unsound mind. Often it was impossible to tell one from the other. The same germ of madness that lies dormant in most people has stirred within a few. During my stay in the hospital, I rubbed shoulders with patients whose behavior on the erratic end of the scale was identical to that of people on the street who were having a bad day. A somber revelation.

* * *

The next day Don, the social worker, dropped in early to see how I had slept. I thought to confide in him my neighbor's possession, his death, and my clash with

202

evil spirits. But when I mentioned the old gentleman's outcry, which had begun the chain of events, Don's interest in my reaction seemed overdone. I felt like a guinea pig. What would his response be if he learned of the spirits? Would he give a report directly to the hospital counselor, a man I had yet to meet? So I guarded my words. In addition, Don seemed overly curious about complaints. Possession by evil spirits was surely a reason for complaint, but what if Don scoffed at the idea of possession? In any case, the Mahanta was using this occasion in the hospital to quicken my appreciation for the Law of Silence.

My intent at the moment was not to reveal anything of a negative quality. When asked how I slept—fine. And breakfast? Couldn't have been better (even though the food and company were uniformly hard to swallow).

Don said that the doctor in charge of my case had switched me to permanent quarters beginning that night. He helped gather my pared-down belongings: shaving kit, the borrowed sleepwear and outer clothing, plus my shoes. It was an easy move; then he left me in my new room.

Soon a female attendant came in with an old man in tow who, she explained, was my roommate. The old gent, lying contentedly on his bed where she had placed him, pretended not to see me, his new roommate—an unwelcome guest. Instead, he amused himself by looking at invisible things on the ceiling and talking to them. With nothing to do, I also lay on my bed and watched the ceiling—unwilling to shut my eyes. After a time, the attendant returned and said, "Come, Henry, it's time for your medicine." He got up and tamely followed her into the hall. Before leaving, the woman said, "If you like, I'll be back in a minute and take you to the library."

Library? If nothing else, I could pass my time there reading books. Despite obvious drawbacks, this hospital might have a few things going for it. And indeed it did. The well-stocked library compared favorably with what might be found on the shelves of any small-town library. The time there passed agreeably, and I hoped to return early the following day.

Next morning, however, Don arrived right after breakfast to tell me of an appointment with the hospital counselor, who was a psychiatrist. The doctor's main office was at a sister hospital in a neighboring city, but he kept a temporary office here for visits twice a week. His office fronted a small lobby that looked out on the parking lot. Don pointed beyond the glass door at a tall man with a briefcase who was approaching us. He limped toward us, aided by a cane. "That's the doctor." As Don spoke, the Golden-tongued Wisdom said to me inwardly, "Psychiatry is an ever-worsening cripple." I tried to block the thought from my mind as Don introduced us, before leaving on other business.

The doctor led me into his office, outside which sat a secretary. Shutting the door, he pointed to a chair for me and squeezed in behind a metal desk. Something was the matter with his left leg, which he favored greatly.

During the consultation, the doctor probed my thoughts in order to pin down the underlying reasons for my behavior. But somewhere he crossed a line that it's wrong to cross. There was an inner side of me, the ECK teachings, which were private. Usually a model of courtesy, he now pressed to understand my spiritual feelings. What did I mean by Sound and Light? Were they figures of speech? And the Mahanta—like Christ? Could I give a personal example of Soul Travel? The man was a professional in that he never poked fun at my experiences, but a discussion with him was like shouting down an empty well and expecting to hear something other than an echo. So many questions; so little understanding. His efforts to repeat spiritual concepts back to me kept coming out like pretzels: hideously twisted out of shape. Unknown to him, his tinkering with the magnificent things of Spirit was creating shabby mutants unique to psychiatry.

Finally, I realized that we were two competitors after the same prize: my inner beingness. But I had a right to command it, whereas he did not.

The interview ended. An attendant escorted me to an occupational therapy room. The woman in charge said, "Look around and do whatever you'd like to do."

In this room were all kinds of things to pass the time: handicrafts, puzzles, games, a typewriter, even painting supplies. I pulled a chair up to the typewriter, intent on beginning the Great American Novel. Sad to say, as so many other aspiring writers have found, the great work was not yet ready to appear. For two days I struggled to write something, even a nonfictional piece, but few satisfactory words emerged on paper. Perhaps it was protection by the Mahanta. Every time I did complete a short piece of writing, the woman pounced on it. "How nice! May I have it for your portfolio?" She, of course, was a direct pipeline to the counselor. By letting me do as I pleased, they could snatch away any products of my imagination for study. I felt like a bug under a magnifying glass. Catching on to their game, I gave up trying to produce the great masterpiece.

Visits to the library were permitted only after I had spent so many hours each day in the occupational therapy (OT) room. My love for reading was used like a carrot, dangling a visit to the library before me if I finished OT. So I began to dabble with paints in the OT room; not that I could pretend at artistic talent, but painting was a way to free the beautiful things inside. So much love to give; so little chance to give it.

Once, during my three-week stay in the hospital, a nurse asked whether I would help her feed a very sick patient. She guided a food cart into a ward and handed me a spoon and a bowl of soup. We went to the bed of an old man who seemed barely alive. He was propped up by pillows, a bed tray in front of him. The nurse put soup on the tip of the spoon and touched his lips. His mouth opened a crack, and she wiped the spoon on the inside of it: one mouthful. Then she left to oversee other helpers feed their patients.

The old man lasted maybe a week. Although unable to speak, his eyes glistened with life. I knew that Soul, trapped inside that worn-out husk, was eager to leave it for good.

Sometimes he showed an appetite. On those days he managed to down a quarter of the soup. Other times he merely tasted it, then shook his head slightly to indicate that the meal was over. So I sat with him in silence. A human in a clinical zoo, he seemed to like having me stop by. But as abruptly as my service had begun, it came to an end. No one bothered to tell me the reason, but I assumed his last visitor had been Death. The day after my transfer from the feeding schedule, I slipped into the ward for a visit, but his former bed was occupied by a new face.

Something about him, however, refused to die and remained with me—the animation and gentleness in his eyes. What kind of a life had he led? A rich one? I hoped he felt no bitterness about ending it in such a coolly dispassionate place.

Twice a week the counselor called me in for a talk. Mostly, on these occasions, he seemed to be a preoccupied individual, a man harried by his own insoluble problems. Don, the social worker, confided to me the fact of the doctor's wooden leg, which was responsible for his pronounced limp. Knowing this made it easier to show compassion, to overlook his encroachment into my domain. My stay in the hospital was thus netting unfoldment in spite of myself. The Mahanta had thrown me into a caldron of individuals with psychological warts: the doctor included. An unconscious desire to understand his own inner workings seemed to have prompted him to choose psychiatry as a profession.

The stay in the hospital was helping me arrive at a new level of spiritual maturity. Although still a child in the wilderness — and probably always, in the sense that unfoldment never ceases — I was beginning to know the real meaning of love.

In fact, most of the patients seemed to have a marked inability to give or receive love. Most of their brothers and sisters — average people on the street — also had problems along that line, but not to the degree found in the hospital. A description that fit the hospital: a haven for people with a fundamentally disturbed need for love. The place was a pressure cooker. A perfect environment for the Mahanta to provide me with sharp, clear insights into people's behavior that would otherwise have taken years to develop under normal conditions. An apt title for this place would have read: Refuge for the Loveless.

One afternoon I learned firsthand how desperate this hunger for love really could be in some patients. I dabbed at a painting in the OT room for a few hours, sufficient to convince the therapist that enough new things were on the canvas to satisfy the counselor. So she gave me permission to go to the library, my favorite haunt. There I could walk through the stacks at leisure, spending an hour to select a book to read in my room after the library closed.

I now had a routine, and life among the patients was quite bearable. It hadn't taken long to determine which patients to avoid, because some had histories of violence. The safest place to spend free time was in the library.

Except this particular day. A volunteer was at the library desk when I arrived. We greeted each other, then I drifted into the stacks for privacy. No one intruded there; no one invaded my space. It was a little corner of heaven, a place to put the pieces together. Being around the patients too much could be a trial. At times, it seemed possible to fall into a strange, uncaring state. There were times I was seriously worried about catching whatever mental or emotional conditions the others had, simply because there was not always a chance to get away to restore myself spiritually.

About an hour later, the librarian came to announce she was going on break for twenty minutes. Would I be OK? It seemed an odd thing to say; after all, this was the library. But she knew more about some patients than she let on. The librarian was apparently not only guardian of the books, but also a chaperone to prevent liaisons between patients in the library. No doubt the staff had good cause for concern.

The library was quiet. The only sound came from the gentle swishing of paper as I thumbed through books. Then came the uncomfortable feeling of someone's eyes upon me. Startled, I looked to my right. There stood Janice, a dead ringer for a woman I knew back in the proofroom. Tall and ungainly, with lean muscles and strong hands, she now wore a queer smile. Suddenly I wondered, *What's she in here for?* Visions of bare-handed violence crossed my mind; certainly she was equipped for it.

Unfortunately, the library stacks in the rear had only a center aisle. Janice was blocking that. My inner alarm bells were ringing wildly. Where was the librarian? Oh yes, on break for another five minutes—if she returned on time.

Janice kept her funny, quizzical gaze on me, not saying a word; I felt helpless, like a turkey on a Thanksgiving platter. She came a foot closer. It was certain she had not come to read. In desperation, I scrambled for a neutral topic of conversation: books.

"Do you often come here to read?" I asked.

Actually, this was the first time I'd ever seen her in here. She was one of those people I had originally sized up to avoid. Now here she was, a sick smile on her face. I turned my thoughts to the Mahanta, hoping for spiritual guidance. As I spoke to her, trying to exude confidence, she hesitated in her slow advance toward me. If only she would talk. That might take the fire out of this volatile situation.

"What is your favorite book?" I asked.

She stared, as if trying to unify conflicting forces within her. But the question had served to stop her from inching closer. Then she seemed to settle into a pool of quietness, as if waiting for inner direction on how to proceed.

Rather than let her deliberation take too long, I added, "Did you hear the librarian come in?" Janice listened. There were sounds in the hall, but it was hard to tell whether anyone had actually entered the library.

"Oh, there she is now," I said, because Janice had once more started to edge closer. "Come, let's have her find you a book." Janice remained undecided, her ear tuned for any movement in the room. Then, as if in answer to my inward call for help, the librarian returned from break.

"Are you still here?" she called out.

"Yes," I replied, "and Janice would like you to help her find a book."

When the librarian heard the name *Janice,* she came directly back to the stacks. Gently, she took Janice's arm. "Come, dear, let's find you something pretty to read." The woman responded to the librarian's gentleness and meekly obeyed. After finding Janice a large illustrated children's book, the librarian telephoned for an orderly. "Janice is in the library. She has a book and wants someone to take her to her room." It was a nice way of saying, "Help! On the double." In no time at all, two men in white clothes came into the library to escort Janice to safer ground.

"I'm sorry," the librarian said. "I shouldn't have left you alone. Things have happened here before. That's why somebody's usually on duty every minute this place is open."

After that, I made certain a staff employee was always close by wherever I went. The patients were here because they did not know how to handle love, or the absence of it.

Later, I thought about Janice as a prototype of the person I knew in the proofroom. The proofreader was also a misfit of love, but she had been more successful at hiding the fact. The experience with Janice, however, taught me to be on the alert for people of that peculiar karmic bent. Under the wrong conditions, they were only a hair trigger from causing harm to others. It was a useful insight, but these lessons for Mastership were almost too graphic for my taste.

Yet my stay was not quite over. The doctor had his own plans for my rehabilitation, and I hoped they would not cause me to lose my independence of mind or spirit. He was the real challenge in the hospital: the social worker, Janice, and all the others were only masks from behind which he worked.

How could I convince him I was OK?

Laughing softly and shaking my head at the incredible question, I replied, "No, I'm not Jesus Christ."

23

"Are You Jesus Christ?"

After my narrow escape in the library from the woman with the unbalanced quest for love, it dawned on me how often the history of mankind revolves around that very same unbalanced quest. Past and modern kingdoms were and are won or lost because of love—or its antithesis, hate. Even the five mental passions — lust, anger, greed, attachment, and vanity—all rise from the absence of divine love.

Another matter related to all this is how some ECKists press to become the Living ECK Master, without any real idea of what that means. They want to leapfrog over the in-between steps to ECK Mastership, certain they have already passed them. Their homemade map to the top of the mountain shows but two points: one, for where the chela is today; the second, for the Mastership tomorrow. They envision a journey bare of rest points along the way. Their spiritual life is like the shell of a book that has a front and back cover, but the story itself is torn from the bindings and lost.

All must walk each lonely footstep to God Consciousness in person. One may bluff himself and others with lowbred ambition, but the ECK and the Mahanta are not deceived by smooth pretension.

Indeed, the end point of all true desire must always be God-Realization. But these times of so much on-the-spot self-gratification have tricked many into believing that something of value can be had without toil equal to its worth. How many people could go directly from the Causal to the SUGMAD world and not be swallowed up by the Fire of God? The plane-by-plane climb has a justification: Since each higher plane is fashioned from a mightier element of ECK, one must inhabit each plane to learn its laws, in order to survive an ever greater flow of life.

Six important events in ECK are these: (1) recognition and acceptance of the path; (2) the Second Initiation, which ends the need for any more physical incarnations; (3) the Fifth Initiation, which sets Soul free from incarnations in all lower worlds; (4) the Eighth Initiation, the last outer initiation at the present time; (5) the Ninth Initiation, where one is accepted as an aspirant in the Vairagi Order; and finally (6) God Consciousness. This is one's admission into a realization of SUGMAD.

Beyond these areas are spiritual beings of still more influence. Among them are the Silent Ones; the Unknown Masters; the Mahanta, the Living ECK Master; and the few who attain the Akshar Consciousness. All these have risen through one branch or another of the spiritual hierarchy, and all range where they will.

* * *

The Mahanta was bringing me up through the ranks, even though he had not yet touched upon my future leadership capacity in ECK. Nor had I ever entertained what would have seemed a most unlikely possibility. My first regard was love for the Mahanta; second, a hoped-for conclusion to my problem with the authorities. In spite of my circumstances, I regarded each moment of life as a blessing. Could it be otherwise?

Some people might argue that my experiences in the Sound and Light up till now were mostly creations of an overexcited imagination. But the fact of Paul's later prophecy about my destiny as Mahanta, the Living ECK Master was to come true. And against fantastic odds.

No one can outmaneuver the ECK in his quest for Mastership. When the experience of God took place for me on the bridge, I had been on the outer path of ECKANKAR only a few years. Besides a chance meeting with Paul at ECK seminars, there was not much physical association with him at all. Yet by degrees, in the next decade, the ECK would draw me closer to Itself. The odds against my being the spiritual leader of ECK were a good million to one, since the SUGMAD might have chosen a candidate from outside of ECKANKAR.

And so, while other visions may also have seemed to outreach my grasp, they too were from the ECK, in which all things are possible. Whatever is the ECK's desire, no might of hell can alter.

* * *

During a meeting with the hospital counselor, he cross-examined me about my splash into the river. Why had I jumped? To commit suicide? Had there been other attempts? The idea of suicide would not leave his mind. Perhaps it was his own fear of water that made suicide by drowning such a compelling idea. But throughout my six years at preministerial school, I had taken Red

Cross swimming lessons, and also a course in scuba diving. The counselor may have had a fear of water, but I did not share his trepidation.

The method he used to probe each of my apparent shortcomings was to arrange a special outing. For example, to test his theory that my jump from the bridge was a thinly veiled attempt at suicide, he scheduled me for a trip to the municipal swimming pool. There, it required no fabulous detective work to guess the attendant's purpose: to observe my self-confidence in water. She kept tossing a volleyball into the deep end of the pool, shouting at me to retrieve it. The first time, when I swam toward it underwater, she had a fit of hysteria. Was I trying to drown? "Swim on top!" she screamed from the pool deck, where she had scurried for a better observation post. So I did. Whatever the outing proved, the counselor did relax his obsession with suicide.

In our sessions, he prodded me to vent feelings of fear or hatred. To pacify him, I gave my all to play the game. Once, in an unguarded moment, when asked my preference for crowds or solitude, I unwittingly chose solitude. Consequently, my next outing was to accompany a group of patients to a movie in town. For that occasion, a dilapidated yellow bus arrived to transport us there. Two attendants, in charge of these thirty patients, asked me to help lead the group from the bus to a side entrance of the theater. This was an interesting turn: to guide others who had acted irresponsibly toward society. Still, in them burned a longing for freedom so often taken for granted by other, more fortunate people.

Roped walkways were set up to conduct our brood through a far corner of the lobby into the seating area of the theater. But when the patients sniffed popcorn, they crawled over and under the ropes and broke for the concession stand. Regular moviegoers, taken aback by the onrush, were driven from their place in line. The attendants, like two cowboys in the middle of a stampede, began to round up the patients, some of whom had headed for the front doors—suddenly intent on a shopping trip downtown. "People in town aren't quite ready for that," a harried attendant explained dryly as she rushed past. The roundup finally saw all the mavericks safely in their seats, eager for the movie to begin.

The quirks of each patient were already commonplace to me from living among them, so throughout the show I was to scan the dimly lit theater for anyone who might bolt for an exit. Then, careful not to cause a riot, I was to diplomatically return him to his seat. It was an afternoon rich in learning.

The counselor, although pleased by the attendants' report of my help in the theater, was still chewing over what significance there might be to my earlier preference for solitude over crowds. Like a dentist trying to replace an old filling, he was anxious to get to the bottom of things, to allow any hidden unsociable behavior to boil to the surface. To accomplish that, he pricked my memory for past events that might have triggered emotional stress. Ever ready to please him and hurry this game along, I pored over my past for an incident that might have sparked pain of the kind for which he was searching. After a long silence, I managed to recall an instance that might appease him.

"Once, in high school...," I stammered.

A smile lit his face; he sat forward in his chair. "Tell me about it," he suggested. Taking out a fountain pen and removing the cap, he poised it over a notepad, ready to capture every biting memory.

"It was my first dance in high school," I began. His pen scratched furiously, then he looked up, waiting to

217

hear more of what he hoped would be a piteous tale of social rejection, the cause of my taste for solitude.

Actually, I'd nearly forgotten the experience. Noting his enthusiastic interest, however, I dressed the story in all the pathos it could bear. Essentially, it was the case of a high-school freshman who got into a predicament because he was ashamed to admit a shortcoming before things got out of hand.

Keith, a classmate in freshman high school, had given me an invitation to his home one particular weekend. When we arrived, he had a surprise: The junior prom at the local high school was that weekend; we would attend. My own little surprise, which I was ashamed to share, was that I couldn't dance. But it was too late to turn back. So Saturday night, his mother drove us to the prom in our Sunday best. While I melted in among the bleachers at the far end of the gym, Keith boasted to his friends what a celebrity he'd brought home with him. Soon he returned, a grin spread from ear to ear.

"You've got the first dance with the prom queen."

In those early years, I had already developed an absolute faith in a higher power to deliver me when things ran amuck. Maybe God'll let me die, I prayed.

No such luck prevailed. An honor guard was formed on the gym floor: a parallel row of boys on one side, girls on the other. The queen was a gorgeous lass who walked with nose aloft. When the signal came to march, we set off between the double row of honor guards, she regally holding my arm. Any second I expected deliverance: to fall lifeless to the floor. But in His hidden ways, God let me reach the center of the gym without divine intervention. When the band began to play for us to dance, I froze.

"What's the matter?" asked her highness.

Shuffling my feet, I said, "I can't dance."

"You can't what?"

In a royal huff, the queen stomped an imperial foot. Eyes ablaze, she turned to a maid of honor, who had rushed up to find the cause of delay. "He can't dance," her highness minced.

A substitute on the sidelines glided in as my replacement. He was a tall, hearty lad with the princely bearing of a football star. Sauntering off the floor with what dignity I could, I retreated to my sanctuary behind the bleachers at a remote end of the gym.

In the meantime, Keith was again busy matchmaking. He found me another date, though much less glamorous than the first. This girl played the violin and wore her hair in tight curls. Yet she was kind. Since she did not dance either, we got along well enough. But ever since that evening, I got weak knees at the mere thought of having to attend a dance.

For his part, the hospital counselor was thrilled to have uncovered what looked like another old sore—still festering— which he was at pains to excise.

News of the annual staff-patient dance came to me by way of the attendant in the OT room. She, by a circuitous route, suggested that the counselor really wanted me at the dance. I blandly ignored her hint. Finally, upset by my purposeful lack of comprehension, she snapped, "Look, do you want to get out of here? Then be there. Understood?" It was perfectly clear that my presence was desired, for there the staff could observe my conduct in yet another social setting. The night of the dance I asked the Mahanta for confidence, then gritted my teeth and danced. The wives of the staff were patient, teaching me elementary dance steps. The event forced me to confront a long-felt aversion to dancing. My hospital stay made me face old terrors. And as I did, they took flight one by one.

219

By now I was growing impatient with the doctor, who still gave no indication of my release date. After accepting his compliments on my behavior at the dance, I asked, "So, when do I leave?"

"Oh, ho, ho," he said with a laugh, "let's not get ahead of ourselves. You're doing well. Keep it up. Another few weeks—who knows?" A classic stall.

About this time he asked about the Mahanta. What exactly did that word mean? "Something like Christ," I answered. It was a parallel he might understand. He nodded, weighed me with a look of appraisal, then dismissed me from his office.

Two days later, Don, the social worker, dropped by after breakfast with outstanding news. "Your staff evaluation is this afternoon."

"What's that?"

"A review of your progress by the counselor and staff," he explained. "If it goes well, it could be your ticket out."

The news seemed too good to be true. The atmosphere in the hospital had a stultifying effect, because a force was always at work trying to control my thoughts and feelings. At times, I wondered how long I could hold on to my rationality. Patients were the counselor's daytime job, but at night he could go home to unwind: by watching TV, eating ice cream, hiding behind a newspaper, loving his family—doing whatever let him mend inside. But all my days and nights were spent in the company of some very unbalanced people. There was no opportunity to relieve tension—as the staff could—by going home to get back on track.

The staff evaluation took place in a conference room. Don accompanied me to the meeting, where I was surprised to find a large gathering of about fifteen people. The seat at the head of the conference table was empty. "That's yours," Don said in a whisper, slipping into the chair on my left. To my immediate right sat the hospital counselor, the psychiatrist. Many of the others were familiar: We'd met in the OT room, the library, the ward, and on the grounds. Only a few faces were unknown.

The doctor led off the questions that traced my history from years earlier, through the night on the bridge, and right up to this staff evaluation. One examiner or another touched upon suicide, antisocial behavior, the possibility of anger toward my parents. They even asked my thoughts about the quality of treatment at the hospital. In every respect, I tried to be fair. By now I had determined that this was the best way to respond. The examiners looked like an open-minded group, so I relaxed, trying to give each question a thoughtful reply.

Finally, the room fell silent. All questions till now, it seemed, had been leading to a central issue, which the doctor was about to broach.

The doctor cleared his throat, then said gently, "There is one thing we'd like you to clear up for us." I nodded, ever cooperative. His great shaggy head turned slowly to take in everyone at the table. Then, giving me a look of veiled significance, he asked the loaded question: "Are you Jesus Christ?"

O Lord, I thought.

I had been resting my foot upon what seemed to be a leg of the table. His question had caught me off guard. Instinctively, I gave the table leg a sharp kick, propelling my chair backwards. The doctor winced and clutched his pants leg. Throughout the meeting, I had unwittingly used his wooden leg for a footstool. Unnerved, I wondered whether the revelation about my footrest or his question about Christ had shaken me more. The faces of the other evaluators were

221

expressionless—impassive and calm. Evidently, the question was a serious one: not a joke.

Laughing softly, shaking my head at the incredible question, I replied, "No, I'm not Jesus Christ."

My low chuckle of wonder grew into outright merriment. It seemed the funniest thing in the world for him to ask that. Had he had a clearer understanding of my ECK beliefs, he might have asked: "Are you the Mahanta?" But no matter how he phrased it, my response would have been no. I didn't think of myself as either a Christ or the Mahanta. His query amused me throughout the rest of the meeting. When the evaluation was over, Don accompanied me from the room. How had it gone? Don wouldn't say. "It's the doctor's call," was all he cared to hazard. I went to the library. The evaluation could only go my way, so I took pleasure in the expectation of freedom. However, things do not always go according to plan. Tomorrow would thus present a further disenchantment.

But it would also bring a searing moment of truth.

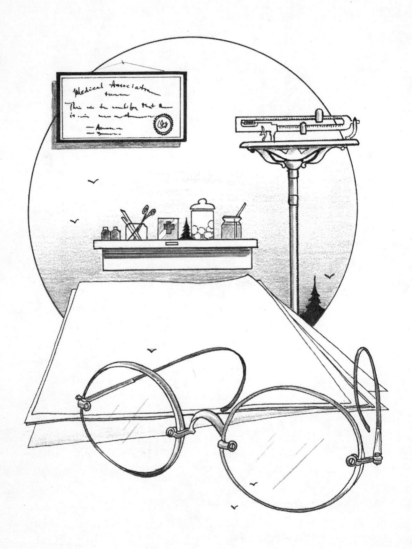

"I'm afraid we're going to have to extend your observation for an indefinite period," he said.

24

Short and Sweet

Someone once said to me, "Life is hard, but I will keep on until I reach God-Realization."

On the surface that is a commendable ideal. His statement, however, carried this undertone: *After I reach the God state, all my hardships will pass and be no more.* Could any idea be more off beam?

The Light and Sound of God are the foundation of the ECK teachings. They, and not any books or scriptures, are the mainstay of ECKANKAR. In his mission, the Living ECK Master meets two complications in dealing with people who want to find God. First, he must acquaint them with God Consciousness as a spiritual ideal; second, he must correct assumptions they hold about its influence on the daily life of one who has achieved it.

People often feel that the Godman is done with learning. After all, is he not able to see, know, and be all? Seen from a spiritual perspective, yes; but physically, no. A God-aware person has simply caught a recognition of his true identity: He now knows his relationship with God. It is a realization—not a belief, not a feeling, nor an understanding. He just knows. He gathered this certainty through the high experience of God, which has transformed him into a perfect carrier of the Light and Sound. From that day on he is an agent for God, delivering the message of spiritual freedom to all who will hear.

Paul Twitchell might have tried to explain the ins and outs of God-Realization to me a hundred times, but I would not have understood. The only real teacher is experience. If lessons seemed to have come swiftly before I met the stranger on the bridge—where the God-experience occurred—they now came nonstop. Before that night, I had unknowingly stored the gleanings of my ECK training in a file called "knowledge of the mind." Since then, however, all experience went into the "hands-on" category. The spiritual transformation that took place on the bridge gave me a whole new outlook on life. It was a changeover that words cannot describe.

Saint Paul, the apostle, gave an apt description of what it means to enter a high spiritual state of awareness. He said, "Therefore if any man be in Christ, he is a new creature: old things are passed away; behold, all things are become new." He was speaking of the Christ state, otherwise called the Krishna, or cosmic, consciousness. Jesus, Krishna, and the Buddha had all entered it in their respective lifetimes. But in ECK, we know of yet higher states, because God's plan always grants a plus element in creation: There is always one more step on the journey to God.

* * *

And so I was learning. Learning how some people manipulate others for enjoyment, and I counted the ways they smoothed over such unprincipled behavior in order to pacify their own consciences. For example, a doctor has no job unless a patient comes to him. But in certain settings, like at this hospital, the authorities had the absolute last word about an individual's future. A hospital administrator knows that patients bring money, whether from private or government sources. To an unethical director, money is money. From my brief stay in the hospital, I concluded that its director sometimes kept too much of an eye on the ledger instead of his patients' welfare. Some patients I met there were more emotionally and mentally fit than their keepers, but they lacked the knowledge or influence to win release.

In addition to an official who might ensure a regular flow of income through keeping the beds in his hospital full, a doctor on staff might decide to run a private study on some facet of a patient's behavior. Who was to stop him? He could delay a release until his curiosity was satisfied. That might take months. This hospital was like a duchy in the Middle Ages: free to run its affairs without too much outside interference.

At least that's how it looked to me.

* * *

The morning after the staff review, I felt good about the chances for resuming my former life. Yet, like a cold shadow, a feeling of dread hung in the air. Finally, I could focus that concern: a flashback to my conversation with the counselor following the dance. When I had pressed him for a release date, he made light of my request, saying it might be another few weeks. But I was confident of my positive showing at the staff review the previous day, which must have changed his mind. Yet maybe I was too quick to forget about accidentally kicking his wooden leg.

At any rate, word came to meet him in his office that next morning. After I had taken my usual seat, he shuffled through a thick sheaf of papers on his desk. ECKANKAR was again on his mind. Why had he not heard of it before? All right, so it was a new spiritual path, but why should I be among the first to join?

He could not understand that it represented truth for me. Through it, I had come to know God's Light and Sound, and no other religious teaching had ever accomplished that before. From my own experience, I knew that ECKANKAR has the breath of living truth.

The counselor seemed to resent a religious ideal based upon a non-Christian teaching. Yes, he would purge ECKANKAR from my thoughts, after which I might return to society—a staid, predictable individual who would pose no further threat to the status quo.

Slowly he removed his glasses and laid them beside his papers, studying me for an endless time. Suddenly, I could sense a readiness to dash my hopes for freedom. Laughing, he shook his head, as if about to do something irrational, something he did not understand either.

"I'm afraid we're going to have to extend your observation for an indefinite period," he said.

At that moment, my future took on a new shape: no more tomorrows, no more yesterdays—only the reality of the living moment. Perhaps the shock of his announcement had achieved in me a practical understanding of surrender to the Mahanta. If one were able to live completely in the moment, he would dwell in the heart of God forever: beyond desire, ambition, fear, or longing.

As had Saint Paul, I was learning to say, "for I have learned, in whatsoever state I am, therewith to be content."

Turning to the doctor, I said, "I have to go along with your decision, but there is something you should know." He raised an eyebrow in mild curiosity, and I finished, "If you brought the president of the United States into this place, how long do you think he'd last before he was like the rest?"

The doctor recoiled with a brief, involuntary movement.

Rising from my chair, I added, "One more thing: you can have me for the rest of my life. I'm going to the OT room to paint."

At peace and no longer willing to play his game of manipulation, I left his office and went to the occupational therapy room, determined to spend the remainder of my days in the pursuit of knowledge.

Unrecognized by me, this conversation had been stirred by the ECK, the Wind of Change.

The horticultural dome sure looked familiar. In answer to my unspoken question he said quietly, "We met there ten years ago."

25

The Unknown
ECK Master Returns

The meeting with the counselor might have been daunting, except I no longer held an opinion about whether the hospital was a good or bad place to be. Wasn't it enough just to be alive?

Time ceased to be neat slices of hours, duties, days, or nights. Everything swam together. Once I sat by a footbridge, trying to capture it with a rude painting. Again, a solitary walk along a dirt path far from the hospital buildings made me aware of watchers, who would return me should I vault the fence to freedom. One whole afternoon I spent talking to a rich, eccentric old man, who sent a threatening letter to the president of the United States every time his release from the hospital appeared imminent. The letter, an automatic extension of confinement for another few years, suited him fine. An extreme penny-pincher, he counted on free room and board at state expense.

As for the counselor, I now regarded him as just an office decoration who required an occasional audience. He was of no more or less consequence to me than the old man. I was starting to enjoy a comfortable life at the hospital: no rush-hour worries; no concern about rent or utilities; no taxes; all food, shelter, and clothing paid for. Maybe the old man was on to something. Here, rich and poor were alike. There were none of the problems caused by ambition—my own or others'. My time was largely my own—to study, to talk with people, and to observe them. Never had I enjoyed such freedom to gather knowledge at leisure.

Then this dreamlike existence vanished like a startled deer in flight. Don, the social worker, dropped by one day to ask if I'd like to accompany him on an errand. This invitation was to determine my readiness to face the big world outside. Pleased by the warmth of Don's invitation, I gladly accepted. That was the turning point; evidently, I had passed the counselor's last test. Plans were being made to find housing and work for me. My old job in the proofroom was still open to me, plus Don had found a room for me in a house run by a Vista worker. But that is a story in itself.

By early summer, I was reestablished as an eight-to-five proofreader at my original job. Independent House, the place run by the Vista volunteer, was an open house for society's outsiders, including Native Americans, parolees, high-school-dropout troublemakers, and even an undercover narcotics agent. Our old house, once ready for the wrecker's ball, had gotten a short reprieve. It was here that I began to rebuild my life around the new consciousness within me. The world, since the experience on the bridge, looked different. Now it was a living thing, pulsing with life, love, and people. But I had to learn how to move within it, without inadvertently bumping into things. It meant starting my perceptions on a new, higher level.

The old breach with my family never fully healed. Every time I went home for a visit, someone would corner me, eyes misting, to ask, "When are you coming back to church?" My life was still ECKANKAR. More than that, there was also this fresh state of consciousness to deal with. I loved my family and understood that their repeated concern for my return to church was really their own fear of hell. How little confidence the church gives some of its children to face the afterlife. But the same is true of some ECKists. Fear is not the domain of any one religion.

That summer, with the God Consciousness intact, I began to test my earlier beliefs gained in ECK. For instance, was drinking alcohol really detrimental to spiritual growth? I decided to find out. For years I had wanted a chance to play baseball or softball for one good season. Like learning to fly an airplane, this pastime of playing ball was very important to me, but circumstances had prevented me from playing it to the point that I could finally say, I've played my best and have no regrets should death come tomorrow. Some might feel it ridiculous to weigh the joy of a good season of ball playing against the finality of death, but something else was at stake.

Life is to be embraced. Unless one has done everything he feels is important, he has cheated himself of the full delight of living. That is a spiritual wrong. Soul can take no material goods into the invisible worlds, only experience. Therefore, if a person feels strongly that a certain course of action would fulfill his life, why not follow it? In ECK, we know that uplifting acts build a better spiritual future, so we try to act with responsibility toward ourselves and others. The simplest formula for doing that is to ask yourself the following questions before proceeding: Is it true? Is it necessary? Is it kind?

In heeding these three points, don't overlook love for yourself. *The Shariyat-Ki-Sugmad,* holy book of ECK, tells us, "Soul exists because God loves It."

The bond between God and Soul is therefore love. Christ said, "Thou shalt love thy neighbour as thyself." This carries love outside the close embrace of God and Soul—to the world around you. How much should you first love yourself if you are to love your neighbor? The Golden Rule defines the extent of that love: "And as ye would that men should do to you, do ye also to them likewise." But judging by how people so often treat each other, it would seem they start with very little love for themselves. Perhaps that's why so little shows toward others.

During that summer I set out to test the effects of drinking upon spiritual unfoldment. That's the stage of life I later called "Spitting in the Face of God." To begin my research, I joined a softball team. The game was only an excuse for what came after it: good fellowship at the local tavern that sponsored our team. The summer slipped away in a happy fog. My drinking companions, cheerful and hearty fellows, were in the same fog. In early autumn, while making a review of my spiritual life, I was dismayed to see how it had slipped back to prehistoric caveman times. No longer could I recall dreams or Soul Travel, both of which had once been spiritual mainstays. Sobered by this decline, I stopped drinking at once and again took up the neglected Spiritual Exercises of ECK.

By now it was Thanksgiving Day. I avoided a trip to the farm because it would have meant a day of fending off well-intentioned religious impositions by some family members. It was to start as a lonely day, as I tried to find an open restaurant, but by day's end a link had begun to form with an event of ten years earlier—my meeting with an unknown ECK Master in Milwaukee near the horticultural dome.

After walking many blocks in the cold, I came upon a place that was serving Thanksgiving dinner. The

234

tables were all filled, but I found a seat at the counter. Beside me sat a hearty man of perhaps fifty. He was reading a newspaper, while a waitress bantered with him about an article in it. The article was about the man, telling of his expertise in raising plants.

"Look at this," she teased. "You of all people—a celebrity!" The man beside me took her kidding in good humor.

As this banter was going on, a dim memory was trying to work its way out of my subconscious. The man's voice was familiar, and so was his craggy face, but it was impossible to place them. The strongest urge came to introduce myself, but to what end? After eating, I left the restaurant and returned to Independent House, which was empty because my housemates had gone home or elsewhere for the holiday. The stranger's face and voice haunted me that night and through the following week. Our chance meeting in that restaurant seemed to have a great emotional pull, more than was called for. About a week later—seemingly by accident again—we met a second time.

There was an out-of-the-way restaurant where on occasion I ran into my uncle, also a black sheep to some in our family. He attended church regularly, and that fact alone should have sheltered him from such treatment, but he liked his beer. No one in our family was a teetotaler, but a few in it were self-righteous about anyone who drank more than they, which my uncle did. Nevertheless, he was a good man, full of laughter and fun.

When I arrived, the jukebox was blaring "I never promised you a rose garden," a line from a country-and-western hit. I got on a high stool at the counter, looking in vain for my uncle. In disappointment, I picked up the menu to order but was startled by the voice of a man next to me calling to the waitress, "How about some pie, OK?" It was the stranger from the other restaurant, the man whose passion for growing exotic plants had resulted in a feature article in the local newspaper on Thanksgiving Day.

The waitress brought him a piece of cherry pie, which he began to wash down with coffee. Again came the strong urge to introduce myself. This time, it would not do to let opportunity knock and go away empty-handed.

"On Thanksgiving I saw you in the restaurant on Wisconsin Avenue, reading the newspaper article about your plants," I said by way of introduction.

He was an expert on succulents, plants related to the cactus family. Every year he created a theme design in his backyard that incorporated the delicate colors of succulent plants. For instance, the design one year might depict national flags from around the world, with succulent plants providing the subtle coloring. His exhibit had become a local legend, with occasional interest shown by the national press.

While he talked animatedly about his succulents, my mind was backtracking its bank of memories, trying to recall where we had originally met, but with no success.

"Come over to my place," he said. "I've got boxes of slides on succulents." That wasn't my idea of a great way to spend an evening, but the inner pull was strong to go with him.

Besides being an expert gardener of exotic plants, he was also a master builder. In fact, he had designed and built his own home. A startling feature about his house was that the back of it seemed to have been turned to face the street. When I commented upon this, he laughed and said, "People build their homes in the strangest way. They put their picture window facing the street. What's out there to see? Noisy cars, loud kids, and unmowed lawns. So I turned my house to face the garden, which makes a whole lot more sense."

His home was of tight construction. Soundproof walls and windows cut street noise to a whisper. The upstairs had been made over into rental rooms for students, who provided him with a steady flow of income, making his home a self-sufficient investment. The Law of Economy ran at an impressively high level in the life of this man.

His large basement was set up like a combination living room, greenhouse, and science lab. A movie screen was already in place at one end of the room, as if he often used it to study slides or show movies. He brought out a handful of boxes containing slides, put them on a table next to the projector, and turned it on. Slide after slide flashed on the screen of one rare succulent plant after another. All the time I asked myself, *Who is this man and why am I here?*

Then a picture on the screen showed a horticultural dome. "Hey," I said, "that sure looks familiar."

His response came in a quiet voice, "We met there ten years ago."

His words struck like a thunderbolt. A curtain that hid the past ripped open to admit the brilliance of an old memory. In that instant, I could again see him a decade earlier in Milwaukee, many miles from here. We had indeed met. The question remained, why? How did he remember me, once a disgruntled high-school senior, now much changed in both appearance and thought? During those past ten years, I had completed four years of college and another four in the Air Force, and spent a year and a half on the farm and better than half a year in town. Counting all that time and all those changes, how did he still recognize me?

"So how do you remember me?" I asked.

Without answering my question, he showed the next slide. He continued with his program as if never having mentioned our first meeting. Upon occasion, an ECK Master may utter a single truth to an individual, then fall silent—to awaken a new understanding.

Lost in thought, I watched the show, reliving our conversation of ten years ago on religion. His prophetic words now came back to me: "In a few years you will find salvation outside your church." That advice turned out as predicted, for since then I had found spiritual liberation through ECK. The record showed that his counsel to finish my education and forget the farm had also been on target. His parting words of ten years ago now loomed in my memory. "You will forget today," he had said, "but we will meet again." Indeed we had.

He shed no more light upon our first meeting than to say, "The past is past. You have much to learn in the present."

Was he really an ECK Master? Who can say? He was planning to move his delicate succulents south to the more hospitable climate of Texas. They would go by rail. I had always wanted to learn about plants from a master gardener. Did he need help in Texas? He was the reason I eventually pulled up stakes in Wisconsin and moved to Texas. But when I got to the town in which he was to relocate, he was not there. No one had heard of him.

In Texas, with no place to go, I headed for Houston—a metropolis with jobs, or so I hoped.

*   *   *

Who was that man? At the least, an agent for the ECK, or Spirit. He had given me a reason to quit my

238

comfortable job in Wisconsin and set out for unknown places.

The day I left, the city was reeling from a snow-storm. My brother came over to say good-bye: a sad farewell. He had always gone out of his way to help me when common sense might have dictated better.

I was determined to live or die within my new state of consciousness, which had settled upon my shoulders like a mantle of gossamer that night on the bridge. God Consciousness did not assure me of a comfortable life, but only of the chance to go on forever as an eternal student of the Sound and Light of God.

That, then, seemed to define my future in Texas.

Nervously, I waited on the leather couch, knowing
that a good job was an opportunity for growth; a bad one, a
modern form of bondage.

26

A New Start in Texas

Behind me lay miles of West Texas dryland, and
the end of an old life. Gone was the comfortable
terrain of home in Wisconsin; here, the partly familiar
land of the Southwest, where I had been stationed at
two Air Force bases.

Yet, the past was past. My old life left no room for
the teachings of ECK. Lutherans at home did not
understand what this otherwise quiet, careful,
thoughtful, and seemingly intelligent human being
could want from ECKANKAR, a new-age teaching. The
neighbors considered my departure from the church an
act of heresy. It had taken a lot of strength to leave the
church, because of pressure from family and neighbors
to stay. Now all that was history.

But beyond my flight from the social consciousness
of the church was a deeper reason that I was not to
understand until later. It was to let the Mahanta help
me unfold so that I could better serve God. For the
moment, however, my attention was on how to pay my
own way; certainly an integral part of self-mastery.

Here, in mid-March 1971, was Houston. I drove into
the city late in the afternoon, and brilliant rays of sunshine

241

blinded me from the sideview mirror. Streams of cars swept around me on the freeway as people rushed home from work. The city had a pulse. It was that of a brash young giant newly awakened to the possibilities of its vitality. A sense of life and living is the impression it made, and in spite of my timidity at running head-to-head with the city at its wildest hour, I steered my car along the vast roads, at one with its commuters.

The future was a blank screen, empty of choices. Would I shovel dirt or build upon my meager experience in printing? A Persian proverb says, "Necessity turns a lion into a fox." Not much the lion, I nevertheless knew it was time to be the fox and hunt for work. Somewhere among this rush of people was a printer in need of a proofreader. But where?

All this time, I had kept up with the Spiritual Exercises of ECK. In reviewing my journals later, there was hardly any mention of outer happenings. It was of dreams, Soul Travel, the Sound and Light, and the Mahanta. Outer insecurity had driven me to the spiritual worlds. Where the world offered little solace or peace, the inner life gave it fully. The teachings of ECK were my anchor in this storm of existence.

And always, there was Paul. Not the man, but the Life Principle of the Mahanta expressing Itself through him. He had been my companion on the journey south. The Mahanta was the silent traveler who did not complain about off-key songs or woeful attempts on the harmonica. He listened to the whisperings of my heart. I lived for the pure love of Spirit that flowed from him.

The trip to Houston had given me a sense of freedom. Self-limitations had begun to fall away; more and more, I felt freeborn. Destiny was mine to forge. Therefore, I would be choosy about employment. My new boss must be a fair man, like George from the Wisconsin proofroom. And the pay should equal my experience.

242

Finally, I pulled out of the hypnotic freeway traffic. The river of vehicles going ever onward made me want to tag along. On the road was freedom. As long as I was moving, problems and doubts were far away, but they caught up with me when I stopped. Stopping meant responsibility, routine, and overbearing people. Yet, society with its trade of goods and services keeps a ruthless scorecard of success: money. Somehow I had to earn money, even though it meant a loss of certain freedoms. The rules were there, and who cared whether I liked them or not?

A sign on a frontage road pinpointed the site of a printing company. But there was no opening for me. A pressman reluctantly gave a lead to another printer. "Here's the name of the company," he said, jotting the information on a slip of paper. "I don't know how you'll like the manager."

Too tired to call on the second printing company just then, I headed for the freeway, where rush-hour traffic had let up. Near Pasadena, a suburb southeast of Houston, I found a motel. It was away from the main roads. Few cars were in the parking lot; tall weeds poked out from cracks in the sidewalk. A damp, musty smell hung in the room, but the bedsheets were clean. Two bare towels and an ant-sized cake of soap decorated the bathroom.

Late the next morning, I cleaned up and had several sandwiches of bread, honey, and cheese—which I had bought the day before at a health-food store. Then I called a few printers from the help-wanted ads of last night's paper, but nobody wanted a proofreader. So I gave up and checked out of the motel. The referral given last night on a piece of paper had both the name of the company and its production manager, Tom. The printer said that Tom was known to be a hard man who expected a first-rate job. Unless his men gave it, he fired them.

The place was hard to find. Nestled on a side street near a major Houston road, the company was in a warehouse with a front office. The white metal sidings were well maintained. The receptionist asked my name, then called the manager over the public address system. Nervously, I waited on the leather couch: choosing the right company was an important matter. A good job was an opportunity for growth; a bad one, a modern form of bondage.

Fast, energetic steps echoed in the hallway from the production area. A lean, handsome man with sharp features burst into the waiting room. His long black hair displayed a careless wave in front and was slicked down on the sides.

"I'm Tom," he said. "What's your handle?" His abruptness startled me, but there was no denying his enthusiasm. "Come on," he said. "Let's see the place."

He led the way into the warehouse where eight units of a web press were in operation. "We print advertising tabloids," he shouted above the din. A crew of pressmen moved quickly around the roaring press. They looked like well-trained seamen on a sailing ship; each knew his job. The presses were grouped on one end of the large warehouse, while the rest of the place was stocked with rolls of paper. On the back dock was an incinerator. The noise was much less there, where two men in ash-smudged clothing fed what looked like perfectly good stacks of advertising tabloids into the fire.

"Idiot printers!" Tom said, his face dark. "A hundred thousand copies with a wrong price." He opened a tabloid to the meat section, which featured beef at the unheard-of low price of fifteen cents a pound.

The grocery chain refused the tabloids, because the error amounted to a handout of thousands of dollars' worth of meat. It was the printing company's mistake, so the grocery chain expected it to make good the loss. The chain was a large regional account, reaching from the East Coast to Las Vegas. From the looks of things, Tom really did need a proofreader. This one mistake alone had cost half my yearly salary in Wisconsin; the error was a point in my favor toward negotiating a good salary.

"Last week we ran bread at two cents less per loaf."

"How'd you get out of that?" I asked.

"I told him we'd cover what he lost in sales. Guess what? Their volume ran that two cents into thousands, so we reran the job. Our best account." Although Tom's job had been on the line, he flapped his arms in a comical imitation of the company president when the latter had learned of the costly mistakes.

Tom led the way past the presses, where pressmen waded through a sea of wastepaper. Knee-deep in places, it made the floor treacherous near the spinning cylinders of the press. Poor housekeeping. One slip and a pressman might stumble into the press. In the industry, horror stories abounded about pressmen who had lost fingers, arms, or hair to a press.

Tom led me to the prepress departments midway between the front office and the press room: pasteup, stripping, and camera. The floor was also strewn with the litter of paper scraps. The stripping room was a dark place illuminated by the fluorescent lights of four light tables. On a stool in front of each table sat a "stripper." This curious name was applied to a worker who stripped down negatives with scissors and taped them to an orange sheet of paper or plastic to make press plates.

This was a strange world for me. At my last job, the proofing department was far removed from the prepress and press areas; it was in a special air-conditioned room on the second floor. Except for an introductory tour at the beginning of my employment, I seldom saw the finishing end of the company's book and magazine products. Thus, the prepress operation here was quite unfamiliar.

"Come to my office," said Tom.

He walked off while I gawked at the bustling of cameramen, strippers, and pasteup artists. "Come on!" he shouted. "Let's not turn into a pumpkin." I caught up and trailed him to his office like a shadow. A couple of months later, when the Mahanta brought me back here for a second chance, the pressmen would call me "Tom's Shadow." By then I would have respect for Tom's skill in management, and understand his fetish for excellence.

But all this was to come. Right now, he wanted to discuss working conditions. "Your proofing table will be at the press," he informed me. He's joking, I thought. My head ached at the thought of trying to concentrate alongside the deafening battery of machines, while inhaling foul press solvents. He dismissed my concern about noise. "In a week you won't even hear the press."

The man was cocky. Deference paid to him by his subordinates bordered on slavish. Nobody fooled with him. Could I work for such a high-handed man?

It was time to talk salary. Tom named a figure: I doubled it on principle. A wild gambler sort of man, he nonetheless lost his poker face at my counter offer. "How much?" he asked, not believing his ears. When I repeated the amount, he whistled. "You're asking too much. The job's not worth that."

The truth was, the scope of this position—assistant production manager—frightened me. My training was in proofreading, not in management. However, this uncertainty brought to light a wavering faith in the

Mahanta, who knew I could grow into the role. Why else had the ECK led Tom to offer it? A fear of having to grow spiritually made me take such a hard line on salary, which lost me the job. My only urgent need, I convinced myself, was enough money to cover simple expenses. However, the real coin of this job was not to be paid in cash, but experience.

We were miles apart on salary. I thought, The Mahanta will provide. He said, "A friend of mine just got out of college. He wants this job, so I guess it's his." Tom's eyes showed a letdown as he saw me to the door. The interview had resolved neither of our needs.

The Mahanta uses every occasion to teach us about life. Though he took me to the perfect job, it did not pan out because of my refusal to accept it. I failed to trust the Mahanta to give the training needed to be a better Co-worker with God. Mistrust and doubt had shut out the Master's plan; it did not fit my perception of one's first duty—to survive. A missed opportunity. It would take further hardships to soften me into a more human being.

As I drove away, a storm was slowly building to the south. The spiritual music of ECK, which had been a steadfast companion from Wisconsin to Texas, had grown fainter as I neared Houston. Only a lingering strain of Its beautiful, enchanting music remained as I breezed along the Houston freeways.

By late afternoon, after many unsuccessful phone calls and interviews, I was beat. Raising an apprehensive eye toward the lightning flashes coming closer, I picked up the newspaper to look for a room. One was listed for only seventeen dollars a week. Feeling small and alone, I dropped change into the slot of a pay phone outside a grocery store and dialed the number.

Not a great start for a new life in Texas.

247

I could see why certain Eastern sages, having lost a few of their illusions about the importance of material things, might choose to sit life out on the sidelines.

27

In Defense of Truth

This was a fine fix. Here I had God-Realization but was struggling to even make a living.

The stranger on the bridge had stripped away the veil of illusion, but it turned out that God Consciousness was not a cure-all in the physical world. The awareness of God gave a deep spiritual insight one could not imagine, but it did not make a onetime proofreader into a financial whiz or anything else.

Indeed, I could see why certain Eastern sages who had attained some degree of enlightenment might sit life out on the sidelines. Having lost a few of their illusions about the importance of material things, they were no longer fit to live in the society of this material world. So they chose to flesh out their remaining years by letting disciples take care of them.

But the Mahanta had a more vigorous plan in store for me. Although he had helped me reach the God state, he now entered me as a neophyte among other candidates for the leadership of ECKANKAR. Instead of being able to enjoy a regular mission as a member of the Vairagi Order, I was again in the ranks of trainees. Once more at the bottom rung, having to scratch out new talents to better assist the SUGMAD. No matter what, I was yet another kind of a child in the wilderness of life, but this time faced with a brand-new kind of discipline and training.

For one thing, who would expect that a common trait like overmuch pride could crowd in upon a God-Realized individual? Yet, it does happen. Difficult-to-manage forces combine to batter anyone who dares to walk the lonely pinnacle of God, but these forces are unknown to all but a few. The road to higher consciousness winds on and on. Beyond God-Realization is found the unimaginable domain of the Akshar. With contemptuous boldness, some people try to play the role of those who are in the Akshar, but even a tenderfoot can see how shameless pride has tricked them on the Astral, or emotional, Plane.

Pride is a scoundrel with a blind-side punch. In my case, I had come to Texas to establish a new life. This effort, however, proved to be an ordeal because of lingering pride. With only a single year of proofreading under my belt, I thought myself above manual labor. But new, more subtle influences of ECK were acting in my life since meeting the stranger on the bridge. Furthermore, it hardly dawned on me that old hangups, like pride, might yet stir inside me.

In defense of truth, let this be said: "The Law of Spiritual Nonperfection holds that no one ever becomes a perfect being." There is always one more step in God's plan of conscious evolution. This is all the more true of spiritual things which always seek, but never find, completion.

But why defend truth? If a grain of sand is the sum of my understanding, why quibble with those who take their bit of sand for a castle? Truth is guarded, given jealously even to its faithful. So it will prove itself.

250

God-Realization, I found, was simply a gateway to new unfoldment; but beyond that gate, things ran in very high gear.

In answer to my written question, the deaf-mute used hand motions and notes to tell me that a thief had stolen his life savings from the shoe box hidden under the bed.

28

The Deaf-Mute

After a few phone calls I found a room in Pasadena, a suburb of Houston. How that came about and how I first met my landlady, whom I'll call Jean, is covered in *The Wind of Change*.

My immediate concern after settling in was where to find work. First, I tried selling a battery additive, then smoke alarms. In both cases I quit, but my understanding of why I quit was only at a *personal* level. In the following experience, the Mahanta gave me another chance to learn the *spiritual* reason behind my apparent failures. He wanted to show me something that was already a part of me, but of which I was unaware. For only by a conscious awareness of this unknown something might I grow spiritually. The lesson was that a spiritual being cannot violate the personal space of others, even if he is desperate to make a living.

After I found a room, the financial roof caved in: my car's battery died, and its brakes failed. The repair of these unexpected, costly breakdowns dropped the floor out from under me. In spite of my best efforts to come up with seventeen dollars for rent, come Thursday my wallet contained a total of twelve dollars. That was all that remained for rent, food, and gasoline.

There was nothing to do but tell Jean, my landlady, the bad news. After supper, the usual time to pay rent, I knocked on the door of her home. She invited me in, but I shook my head. "I can't pay the rent."

"Well, come in anyway," she said. "It's not the end of the world."

Jean had an interest in ECKANKAR. Every week she asked about dreams or Soul Travel. Her own dreams were vivid, so she liked to share them. Two weeks after my arrival, she had reported seeing me several times in her dreams. "I pray for you," she said, but I told her that the Mahanta was taking care of my spiritual life. However, Jean was developing her powers of prophecy. "There are great things in store for you," she said. I did not tell her, but the very day of her prediction, the Mahanta had taken me to Agam Lok, the inaccessible plane. It was part of my training to later wear the spiritual mantle of ECK.

In that journey into the pure spiritual planes of God, the Mahanta and I walked further into Agam Lok. There hung a fathomless rope. "There is the rope, Master," I called. I looked at it with wondering eyes, as if for the first time, though I had been here before. Quietness reigned. No time or space separated us from the worlds below. The nearness of all worlds seemed wonderfully clear: No past, present, or future in a conventional sense. All there was, was *now;* the eternal moment.

During our brief acquaintance, Jean and I had come to respect each other's spiritual beliefs. "Forget about rent," she now said. "Just get on your feet. Do you have enough food?"

After reassuring her about the food, I went out for a newspaper. I vowed to take the first job that came

254

along. One ad in the paper caught my eye. It advertised for young people who were free to travel. An unlimited opportunity to make big money—fast. The ad was speaking to me. I dialed the number from a pay phone, and a young man named Bernie answered. He gave few details about the job. After a short conversation, he asked to interview me at home tomorrow. This was all too quick, but what was there to lose?

Home again, I knocked on Jean's door and told her of the call. Tomorrow, after the interview, I would tell her all about the job and when she could expect rent.

The next morning I was up early, anxious about the interview. At eleven o'clock sharp, a station wagon pulled into the driveway. The driver was hardly more than a boy; he went to Jean's door, because that looked like a home. She directed him to my garage room, where I waited for him in the doorway. His name was Bernie, and his eyes took in my living quarters at a glance. My room was not the most impressive place: it looked like the refuge of a person on his last dime. The rug had once been soaked in a hurricane, giving the room a strong, musty odor.

Bernie was seventeen. Still too young for a valid driver's license, he was nevertheless proud of his forged one. He and a troupe of magazine salespeople followed the seasons around the country. In summer, they roamed the northern cities; in winter, the warmer climate of the South.

His team traveled first class, he said. They stayed in the best hotels. Food was charged to their account and later deducted from monthly sales. Under the circumstances of my poverty, the job seemed an excellent way to earn some quick cash. But there was a catch—for some reason he did not want to hire me. He had a graceful method of dropping a prospect who was not cut out for the sales team. Bernie's manager, whom I would meet later, insisted that interviews be held in the prospect's home. This way, if the person seemed wrong for the position, Bernie could end the interview and disappear.

"When do I start?" I asked.

"You've got the qualifications," Bernie said, "but our team's moving out of town in two hours." Two hours. A way of saying, "We don't want you." Who could just drop everything and say, "OK, hold on. Be with you in a minute"? But I did.

Bernie stood in the corner by the door, watching in disbelief while I packed my suitcase with clothing and vitamins. Then I went to tell Jean of my plans and ask where to park my car so it would be in no one's way. Ten minutes later, fully packed, I locked the front door and got into the station wagon with Bernie, who did not look happy at all.

A long drive took us to a suburb at the northwest end of Houston. Bernie stopped at a motel and introduced me to the other members of his team: six young men and women. Bernie was the youngest; the others were eighteen to twenty-five. He took me to a large room with a king-size bed.

"You sleep here with Fred and Richard."

So this was the first-class life—three of us in one bed. I began to miss my own, without even having spent one night in this "grand" place. Bernie outranked us, so he had his own room. All in all I fared pretty well, securing the right side of the bed, rather than the middle, where I would have been flanked by strangers.

"Wake-up's at six," said Fred, rolling over to sleep.

After passing a fitful night, I awoke a few minutes before the alarm to take vitamins, which had become a part of my regime a few months earlier. My stomach was upset because the life-style of these people was so different from my own. Sleeping three to a bed did not approach my standard of luxury. Later, I learned that these young people, for the most part, were servants of the sales manager, with little to say about living conditions.

Breakfast was a joyless occasion. Bernie showed me what I could order from the restaurant's menu: the smallest, cheapest portion of eggs and toast. He picked up the tab on our way out, to demonstrate the generosity of our employer. Of course, the cost of meals would later be taken from our sales.

Broke, except for a paltry twelve dollars, I felt terribly lonesome—forsaken by the Mahanta.

With breakfast out of the way, it was time to earn our keep. Like hired hands ready to attack a field of harvest, eight of us packed into the station wagon. With Bernie at the wheel, we drove to a nearby suburb. Later, I learned that we were but one of several teams working out of that motel. Like grasshoppers landing in a garden, each team was dropped off in a carefully mapped neighborhood of a suburb.

The people from our car headed in every direction. Bernie watched them leave, then the two of us drove a few blocks further, where he had told the others to meet for the lunch pickup.

As we started up the sidewalk of a home, Bernie pointed to the family name on the mailbox. "Come with me," he said. "You'll learn the ropes."

The home was surrounded by tastefully arranged trees, shrubs, and flowers. Bernie knocked on the door, then whispered, "Watch." It was not by chance that Bernie was team leader. He had a reputation for separating people from their money in a coolly efficient way.

A woman of refined manners answered the door. Soft brown hair curled forward to touch her kindly face.

Bernie launched into his innocent-child-with-wide-eyes-out-in-the-big-world-for-the-first-time sales pitch. It was uncomfortable watching him push into the gentle world of this woman.

"Hi, Mrs. Jones," he said, giving the name from the mailbox. "I just came over to see you for a minute. I don't know whether you know me or not, but my name is Jeff. And what I came over for is to get you to back me up in this year's district Savings Bond Contest. You haven't backed any of the other guys yet, have you?"

Bewildered by his machinegunlike burst, she shook her head.

"Swell," he continued, "then I'll be the first one to tell you all about it and get you to back me up. You do have a couple of minutes I can get you to sit down and explain it to you, don't you?"

A minute later, we were seated in Mrs. Jones's living room. Two high-school girls entered the room and sat on either side of their mother on the couch. Then Bernie went to work in earnest, with no more mention of savings bonds. He whipped out a brochure of magazine titles from his back pocket, then badgered the family until the poor woman agreed to buy a magazine. Still he drove on, trying for yet another sale. The poor woman's face showed distress, but she was too gracious to insist upon our leaving.

Bernie was facing the mother, so he could not see me giving her eye signals. While he pitched the second magazine, I caught her eye and shook my head. Bernie saw her look past him and turned, but I wore a mask of bland indifference. Finally, Bernie realized that she was not in the market for another subscription. Mrs. Jones saw us to the door. As we turned to go she looked at me, giving a barely perceptible nod of thanks.

I did not like what had happened. Were the other team members as hard-driving as Bernie? If so, I wanted out; no amount of money was worth that.

Bernie next went to an apartment complex and stopped at the mailboxes. "Always get the name of somebody who lives here in case the manager catches you," he advised. As luck would have it, the apartment manager met us on the stairs leading to the second floor. He was an older man with a knowing look.

"No soliciting," he ordered.

"We're here to visit Mrs. Wolf," Bernie replied, without a blink. The manager, caught off-guard, said, "Sure, she's in 202. Of course, you know that."

But Mrs. Wolf examined us through her security peephole and in a muffled voice announced that she did not want to buy whatever we had to sell. Bernie tried a few more doors with the same luck. Fortunately, it was eleven o'clock and time for lunch. I wondered how much longer I could continue this charade.

After lunch, Bernie assigned me to Linda, a top seller on the team. She was to add another dimension to my training. Bernie came on like a fresh-faced kid in high school, but Linda played the role of a young woman on her first job. She made believe that selling for her was a half-fun, half-serious game that all too soon would bow to a more staid profession. An altogether believable act. As a bonus, the prospect was to learn that the sales contest might also win Linda a trip to Hawaii. Her airy manner cajoled customers into helping her win the contest. Her easy approach almost made me reconsider my growing dislike for magazine sales.

It was nearly three o'clock, an hour from quitting. "Why don't you try your hand on the next mark?" she asked.

"I'm not ready," I said.

"The only way to learn is by doing," she insisted. "Now do it."

She poked at the doorbell. A young man opened the door. He reminded me of Rebazar Tarzs, famous ECK Adept from Tibet, who sometimes traveled with me on the inner planes. This man's accent was crisp and pointed, like Rebazar's. Before we could open our mouths, he said, "So how do you know I want what you're selling?"

Linda did not like anyone getting ahead of her. She wanted to direct the conversation, but already he had us on the defensive.

"Let us in, and you'll see," she retorted.

"Just get to the point," he said. "I work tonight."

Nevertheless, he swung the door open to let us in. The furniture in his apartment was of high quality, with a striking and elaborate stereo system in place. In addition, his housekeeping was spotless.

I began my halting presentation. Groping for the right words, I told him of his chance to help me win a trip to Hawaii.

"So you fly away to Hawaii and have a good time; I stay in Houston. What kind of a deal is that?"

Now Linda came into the game. With a winning smile, she said, "Carl and I just started selling these wonderful magazines, but I'm sure you already know all about them." Slowly, she began to weave her web. It became a personal thing to sell him at least one subscription. All the while he listened to her with a bemused look.

"All right, I give up," he said. "If nothing else, you've earned it. I sweat for my money and don't like to see people get it too easy." To my surprise, he wrote a check.

"I'm sorry I have to work now," he said. "I've never heard so many good reasons why I should send perfect strangers to Hawaii." There was a glint of humor in his eyes, but Linda looked worn out from her effort at making the nearly impossible sale.

When we reached the street, Linda turned on me, her eyes blazing. "You're not going to make it. Start selling or you're gone."

"I can't just take money from people," I said. "Do they ever get their magazines?"

"If you want to stay around, you'd better sell," she repeated. "Who do you think pays for lunch?"

The last forty-five minutes had netted her just one sale, far too slow. So she sent me off alone so she could try for a few more sales before quitting time. "Try that place yourself," she suggested, pointing toward a small apartment complex on a side street.

Reluctantly, I made my way toward the brown building. Addressing the Inner Master, I asked, Why is it all so hard, Paul? But no response. In my darkest hour, the Mahanta seemed to be nowhere about. There was no alternative but to try my hand at selling. After all, this was the job which the Master had provided, whatever the reason.

At the mailboxes out front, I memorized a name in case of a challenge. Then I walked toward the staircase, passing a room with its door ajar. Gingerly, I stepped up and knocked. Getting no answer, I knocked louder. The door opened partway, revealing a small room; an empty shoebox lay on the bed. The rest of the room looked chaotic, as if someone in a rage had dumped the dresser's contents upon the floor. There was an incompleteness about the scene: Where was the owner? Why had he, or she, left the room unlocked and untended?

Selling magazines was very much on my mind. I had to sell to pay for my meals and room. That much was clear from Linda's angry outburst.

Just as I started to go next door, a terrible wail arose from the far end of the building. Toward me stumbled a squarely built man, whose face was wet with tears. He dabbed a soiled handkerchief at his perspiring bald head. Stopping in front of me, he gestured wildly with his hands. Something awful had happened. But his sobbing made it impossible to understand a single word. He brushed past me to enter his room, then emerged immediately, wailing louder than ever.

"What's going on?" I asked.

Pointing to his tongue, he shook his head and pulled a pen and notebook from his shirt pocket. Holding them out to me, he motioned for me to write. Slowly it dawned on me: he was a deaf-mute. Impatient with my hesitation, he wrote, "What do you want? Write," then thrust the pen and notebook toward me again.

By this time, the confusion had me dizzy. So I wrote, "I'm selling magazines. Do you want to buy some?"

He took back the notebook, studied the note, then his eyes went wide. Looking at me as if I were mad, he let out a shriek. Weeping helplessly, he buried his face in the handkerchief; I put my arm around him. In a little while, he calmed down. Writing in my own notebook, I asked, "What's going on?"

Glancing at my question, he led me by the arm into his home. Using hand motions, notes, and broken sounds, he indicated that a thief had broken in and stolen his life's savings, which were hidden under the bed in a shoe box. He sank down on the bed while I went off to find help.

Several doors away was the manager's apartment. With some misgivings, I knocked on the door. What if the manager accused me of the theft? The smartest thing to do was to hoof it out of there. Anyway, it was time to meet the pickup car; in fact, I was late. It might be some time before the deaf-mute could tell someone of his loss. By then, I would be far away. Instead, I found myself knocking on the door of the manager.

A wisp of a woman opened the door. When I explained the tragedy of the deaf-mute, she invited me in while she called the police. I told how I had found him a few minutes earlier, but also that I was late for my ride.

"I understand," she said. "Thank you for taking the trouble to help him. He doesn't have many friends."

This experience did it: forget magazine sales. It would be better to starve than face another such person in trouble, while my objective was to relieve him of whatever money I could. Hurrying to where Bernie had told us to meet at four, I berated myself for trying to sell a magazine to a person who had just lost his life's savings.

The street along which I walked was empty and narrow; no cars were parked there. It seemed to be a midway point between the outer and inner worlds. Then toward me came the familiar figure of a man, the same man to whom Linda had sold the subscription.

"Still getting rich off other people's misery?" he asked, with a disarming smile.

"This is my first and last day with them," I said. "I don't know who they are or where they're from. I don't even know if you'll get your magazine. I need money, but not that bad." When I told him of the deaf-mute, his eyes softened. "Do you have a place to stay?"

"That depends on whether they take me back to the motel."

Then he reached into his pocket and took out a key. "This is for my apartment," he said. "Stay there if you want. I'll be back later."

His generosity floored me. "You don't even know me."

263

He waved a hand in a sign of dismissal. "You're welcome to stay."

"Thanks," I said, refusing the key. "I'm OK now."

He smiled, then crossed the street. It seemed odd, but there was no place for him to go: this was a residential area. In his room earlier, he had told us he had to be at work by four; it was now nearly five. So I took his intervention as a sign of the Mahanta's presence, helping me in the guise of another Soul.

Bernie drove up. Everybody was already in the car. "Where were you?" he demanded. "We want to get back."

"Selling's not my thing," I answered. "It may be right for you, but not for me." I told of meeting the deaf-mute, and how that experience made me want to try another line of employment. The team members began to open up when they heard about the deaf-mute's misfortune. At least they had an inkling of my feelings.

Back at the motel, I met the sales manager. He looked like a petty mobster, complete with sunglasses. A rough-looking man stood beside him as I asked to leave the team. "I can't rob people."

"Get out!" he thundered. "You walk home."

Dejected, I went outside. Night had fallen. The lights were on in the parking lot. The members of the team asked what the manager had said. When they learned he wanted to abandon me, Linda and another girl stormed inside. The other young people cast anxious looks through the window, where the two girls were in a heated debate with the manager. Finally, they came outside, triumphant smiles on their faces.

"He said Bernie will give you a ride when he gets back from an errand," Linda informed me. I offered my thanks; we said our good-byes. That night, back home, I stopped to tell Jean of my day. No matter what, I had to respect the rights of others while pursuing my own livelihood.

That was the lesson the Mahanta had set out to teach me.

I did all sorts of unpleasant manual labor, for the Mahanta saw that I did not entirely understand how important responsibility was as a balance for freedom.

29

Turnabout in Texas

What I was learning about God Consciousness was that though the world may be seen through a new set of eyes, the same old battle for survival exists. So then, what was different about life? What made it more worth the struggle than before I had met the stranger on the bridge?

For one thing, I now knew with certainty that life proceeds in orderly cycles. A downhill run can go on a long time when a person is caught in the vise of karma, but once spiritually awakened, he can draw upon resources beyond imagination and change direction. He knows a downhill slide can be made to end. Yet even someone with God Consciousness must deal with cause and effect, because that is the way of the lower worlds, which range from the Physical to the Etheric planes. Call it karma, if you will, but any act always triggers a response, whether seen or not. This opposition of forces is the balance in life.

With this principle in mind, one is gladdened by the Mahanta, who is ever ready to open doors for Soul, to show a path where only thorns would seem to flourish.

No matter how bad things got, I knew brighter times were ahead. Several attempts at sales had nearly ruined my self-confidence. In turning me away from selling, the Mahanta was trying to show me how to build upon previous experience in printing, to give me a background in printed communications. That knowledge was crucial to my later responsibilities of presenting the message of ECK.

With sales out of the picture, my money gone and no openings in proofreading, I went to an agency to apply for temporary work. The specialty of this agency was manual labor—and often the most foul clean-up jobs that clients would not ask of their own employees. Thus I unloaded pesticides from steaming boxcars, cleared brush for a massive housing development, washed floors at the San Jacinto monument, choked on dust while cleaning up an enormous grain elevator, and many other such assignments. In the process I got sick from chemicals, contracted poison ivy, and fell from the top of a warehouse ladder.

But early every morning I entered the office of the temporary agency the minute the doors opened. I couldn't afford to miss a single day. My pay barely stretched to cover gasoline, rent, and the small amount of food I ate. There was just enough money to come back tomorrow, but never enough to break free of this deadlock and rise to a better life. But I held on.

What accounted for my fall into these conditions? The Mahanta, the Living ECK Master was preparing me for the leadership of ECKANKAR. He saw that my understanding of freedom was still inadequate. Despite the experience of God—which many wrongly accept as a perfect state wherein one intuitively knows all things without the need to go through experience—I did not entirely understand how important responsibility was as a balance for freedom. So many people fall for the same error. The Master had led me to a job almost the day of my arrival in Houston, but I refused it; now, a third of the salary offered would have served my needs well. The Mahanta's point was that experience is always worth more than money. During this shortfall of money, I surely did get plenty of experience.

One day, the clerk at the temporary agency posted an assignment for operating an incinerator at a certain company. The old hands in the waiting room shook their heads in refusal, for this was summer in Houston, a hot and muggy season: not the time to feed an incinerator. Nevertheless, I volunteered for the job and signed a paper. The clerk coaxed two others to join me, whereupon I drove us across the city to a large building and parked in the employees' parking lot. We went inside, dreading what we would find.

To my surprise and delight, it was a printing company. From my vantage point just inside the employees' entrance, I saw a new warehouse. The half nearest us was stacked with rolls of printing paper, and in the background howled a web press, with rolls of white paper streaking through its cylinders, taking on ink.

What a glorious feeling. And the smell of solvents and ink. I felt as if I had come home. Like a captain on his quarterdeck, I stood braced with legs apart, hands on hips, taking in the wonderful sight. I was suddenly alive. This was joy. Who else could understand? Laughing, as if I owned the place, I went up to the press and watched the pressmen scrambling nimbly around their machine like sailors rigging and tending the sails on a ship.

"You from the agency?"

Someone was shouting into my ear. I looked around and saw a printer in an ink-soiled grey uniform, gesturing me away from the roaring press. He led the way to a loading dock, which was jammed with pallets of printed circulars.

"A printing error in price," he explained, no longer having to shout. "They all go into the incinerator."

The job was mammoth. The incinerator had a wide mouth, and I stuffed as much paper into it as it could hold at a time. The other two men from the agency were given tasks inside the air-conditioned building, while I labored in the heat. But I was happy. I felt like a king returning to his kingdom after a long absence. By day's end, I had cleaned up the mess on the loading dock.

My supervisor, impressed by the speed and quality of my work, asked me to return the next day. His invitation did not include the other two men.

The following day, the supervisor put me alongside the press. Thousands of shopping flyers spilled from its folder each hour. My job was to gather, then bind them into small, easy-to-handle packages, and stack them high on pallets. In the morning, a shipping firm would load the pallets into a semitrailer for delivery to customers anywhere from Nevada to the East Coast.

It was an art to stack bundles of flyers on a pallet. First, the bundles had to be interlocked in certain patterns to provide stability so they wouldn't fall off. Second, they had to be stacked so they formed a straight wall on each side of the pallet. Otherwise, the load might still shift and topple, causing both damage to the flyers and a delay in shipment.

The roar of the press was deafening, yet I was happy to be there. I felt a kinship with these pressmen, even though as a proofreader in Wisconsin I had seldom been able to visit the production department. An old printer's joke came to me as I stacked pallets: "Once I couldn't even spell *printor,* but now I are one."

Because of my newness on the job, I sometimes lagged behind the press. A pressman would then leave his usual duties for a few minutes and help me catch up. But no matter how far I fell behind in stacking pallets, I always took care to build ruler-straight sides.

A soundproof bay window in the pressroom manager's office commanded a view of the pressroom. The first time I glanced toward the window, two men stood in the office, peering toward the press. Meanwhile, the pallets I had stacked looked square when compared to others. About ten minutes later, a few more people had come to join the first two men at the window. A half hour later, more people had come and filled the room. Some, shaking their heads as if in wonderment, pointed in the general direction of the press.

Finally, the press run, which numbered over two hundred thousand copies, came to an end. Pressmen, agile as monkeys, replaced old printing plates with new ones, washed blankets, and put fresh rolls on the paper stands. Then everyone took a breather: a lull in the storm. From a vending machine, I bought a soft drink and drank it by the folder, ready to begin work when the presses rolled.

From the office there now emerged a big man, wide in girth, but with a pleasant face. I guessed he was making a walk-around inspection during break, but to my astonishment, he came directly to me.

"Those are the straightest skids I ever saw," he said, beaming a broad smile and pointing to the pallets.

"Thanks. I do what I can."

"You wouldn't be looking for work?" he asked. "What's your line?"

Startled, I replied, "Proofreader."

Now he looked startled. From my own experience in the job market, a proofreader in Houston was a rare

271

bird. I had discovered that sobering fact during my unsuccessful job hunt after refusing the job at...Wait! Suddenly, this place looked familiar.

Then it dawned on me. It was here at this very place, the day after my arrival in Houston, that I had refused a job from Tom. On that day so long ago, I had parked in the visitors' parking lot, come through the front door, and spent most of my time being interviewed in the front office. Tom had taken me on a lightning tour of the pressroom, but everything looked different now. This time I had come in the back way, without ever seeing the front office. Many weeks had passed since my arrival in Houston; therefore, it was no wonder I had forgotten that initial visit.

The odds of returning by chance to this particular company were immense. It was one of many thousand companies tucked away in the vastness of Houston and its suburbs. To better understand the odds, it was an assignment by an indifferent clerk in a temporary employment agency that had landed me here. Chance had not been the agent for my return: From past experience, I knew the hand of the Mahanta was all too evident. He remained willing to guide me into a broader, more productive life. To attribute to chance my happy return to this company would be a foolish disregard of the evidence at hand. The months of hardship since I first declined the Master's gift had taught me to quickly recognize and appreciate his smallest favor. Life had far greater treasures to offer than money.

Did I want a job? Of course!

"You won't believe it," the pressroom manager said, "but we're running an ad for a proofreader. Come this way, please."

Without a word about salary, I had accepted his offer. He took me from the pressroom into the front office and handed me an employment form. A few minutes later, I was a company employee. Just then Tom, the production manager, walked into the pressroom manager's office. I recognized him right away. Now that I remembered where I was, all the pieces of my first visit fit into a complete picture. Fortunately, Tom didn't remember me. His friend, the budding proofreader who was to get the job I had turned down, had quit a week after being hired: He couldn't tolerate the noisy press. Since then, the company had had as much trouble finding a proofreader as I did finding a proofreading job. In the meantime, both Tom and I had gained a larger degree of give-and-take. This time around, we tempered our demands and made allowances for each other. To my satisfaction, he had now set the proofing table in the front office, away from the noise of the pressroom. Months later, when he finally recognized me as the person of that first, unsuccessful job interview, he was pleased with the value he got for the salary he paid.

For a little over a year I remained in Houston. During that time, the Mahanta showed me many things about the operation of creation and survival.

And then, it came time to leave.

The act of beginning to write this story had unleashed a grand wave of positive energy, causing an outer storm to manifest.

30

About This Story

O nce again did the Wind of Change, the ECK, stir within me. I was now the assistant production manager at the printing plant in Houston, in charge of both the afternoon and midnight shifts. The people here had come to trust my record for dependability and ingenuity. But Texas was closing out for me. The ECK was nudging me to find a greater spiritual expression in some other place.

About that time, the manager of the ECKANKAR Office in Las Vegas wrote to ask if I would like an interview for a job in printing. Ready to sail with the Wind of Change, I felt the breath of new opportunity in the air. After a month's notice to my employer in Texas, I loaded my car and drove to Las Vegas. Finally, it seemed, I would be able to work near the Living ECK Master. But to my chagrin, the manager hired someone else in my stead, a person who later left ECKANKAR. Stranded in a glitzy show town without a job, I further learned that the prospect of finding work was slim.

Here was the downbeat of a familiar cycle that had so often dropped me to a life of bare-bones existence; I knew its old melody by heart. But yet another set of miracles intervened to land me in the printing department of what was then the largest hotel in the world, saving me once more from the uncertainty of poverty.

It was while in Las Vegas that I first tried to write this account of how I had touched the Face of God. I felt that perhaps in reading my story, someone else would find the inspiration to seek his own path to the Boundless Source of All Being, the SUGMAD.

My room then was in the home of a real-estate agent and his wife. The ovenlike desert air caused me no discomfort in summer, partly because shade trees surrounded the house, and also because some thoughtful person had painted the walls of my room an azure blue. This gave the feeling of a cool place by the sea. In addition, the windows were small, placed high near the ceiling. Mostly, however, credit for the cool temperature belonged to a hefty air conditioner. Woodwork in the room was creamy white, which, accented by the azure blue and the coolness, truly lifted the spirits of anyone who entered. Furnishings included a twin-size bed, a refrigerator and a hot plate, a closet, shower room, and a card table by my bed on which rested my ancient typewriter with the crooked letter *t*.

It was here, late one Saturday morning, that I intended to begin writing this story. Just home from doing my wash at a coin-operated laundry, I was glad to escape the scorching breath of the Nevada sun. My typewriter seemed to beckon from its roost, so I quickly packed away my clothes and put a sheet of paper into the platen. Typing steadily, I lost all track of time or place as I went back along the Time Track to relive the events related in this book—especially the experience on the bridge.

The hours flew by. Suddenly, I was jolted from my reverie by a bright flash of lightning and a peal of thunder. Immediately, there followed the drumming of hail on the roof, and a downpour of rain came right behind. Brilliant stabs of lightning illuminated my room, while a savage wind whipped the trees outside the windows. This was unusual. Storms of this intensity seldom hit Las Vegas. I jerked the plug from the wall to prevent a bolt of lightning from disabling the typewriter. To watch the storm, I climbed onto a chair to look out the high windows. All that was visible through the rain-splattered glass was the lashing branches, as the wind seemed intent on ripping them from the trees. The storm was a magnificent sight.

Then the reason for the storm came to me: The act of beginning to write this story had unleashed a grand wave of positive energy. The mere retelling of a God-Conscious experience has a tremendous impact upon the spiritual community of the world: It causes the very ethers of creation to tremble.

As I had been pounding out the account on my typewriter, a great spiritual energy was released that ran head-on against the normal, everyday vibrations over Las Vegas. This caused a terrible collision between the ECK and Kal forces. Like a cold front overtaking hot weather, the inner clash of positive and negative forces caused an outer storm to manifest.

Overwhelmed by the splendor of the raging storm, and not able to continue typing anyway, I made a dash for my car. Slowly I drove along residential streets, watching trees bow before the gale. *This is my handiwork,* I thought, not a little in awe. Electrical wires were down, but the fury of the storm did not abate. It then occurred to me that it might yet be too soon to record the events of that night on the bridge. Carefully I drove home through the debris-ridden streets and tore the typed pages to shreds, flushing them down the toilet. That done, I returned outdoors to see the storm clouds retreat before the sun.

This story has been long and hard in the telling. A few years ago I gave a talk at an ECK seminar, using the title of this book, because I had again begun work on this manuscript. But that was not the right time either. So it was shelved until now.

Even this attempt nearly did not reach completion. The ECK came through so strongly during this past year of writing that the Spiritual Power often burned my inner bodies. Worse still, my wife was acutely aware of whenever I worked on the book. From her desk in another part of our home, she often mentioned feeling as if she were on a slow roaster. Nor did our little dog fare much better. Whenever I began to labor over the keyboard of my computer, she got restless and refused to settle down, making it hard to concentrate on the writing. These, and many other things, cropped up during the months of writing this story.

Only now, at the conclusion, have I noticed a diminishing of the burning sensation caused by the power of ECK.

I mention all this simply to acquaint you with the surety of the ECK Power. While ECK, Divine Spirit, is certainly love, it is actually the blending of spiritual love and power that purifies all who read these words with open hearts and minds.

* * *

How can one in all modesty write about God-Realization? One such telling is in Paul Twitchell's *The Tiger's Fang; Child in the Wilderness* is another. Whether or not the majority of people believe these accounts is hardly important. However, if the narrations inspire even a single individual to reach the

278

Godhood inside himself, the effort required to describe these experiences will have been worth the while.

Relating this story presented a knotty problem. A story can be told in a variety of ways, but I like to put the most interesting and significant event last: The story tells better. In this book, then, that would have been the chapter entitled "The Experience of God." But this book is also to address misconceptions about what happens to a person after he has reached the high point of all his lives, or the God state. Life does not always unfold like a good story, which builds toward a climax with all ends neatly tied up.

Therefore, the events in this story consider not only what preceded, but also what followed my experience of God-Realization. And that experience is lodged somewhere in the middle of the book. The story runs like a curved line that rises from the bottom of a page to the top, then goes down the other side. It starts at the bottom, on a plain—as a regular story might—and goes to the top of the hill. But instead of ending there with God-Realization, as one might expect, the storyline continues down the hill until it again reaches the plain of everyday living on the other side.

The necessity of showing this protuberance of God Consciousness in the center of the book was used as a teaching device to show how life really works. Thus, even the structure of the book is a graphic example of one's rise to the top of the Mountain of God, but also his descent again into everyday life, which is never the same as before. A God-Realized person enjoys the privilege of being a Co-worker with God.

To complete my story, I went on to become the Mahanta, the Living ECK Master. That is the subject of *Soul Travelers of the Far Country*. This rise to the spiritual leadership of ECK fulfilled the prophecies of several ECK Masters, including Paul Twitchell.

* * *

By now, you realize that only a feeble description is possible of the God-Conscious experience. It may happen in the way it did to me, or one may find the circumstances to be of an entirely different sort. Who can say beforehand? The Mahanta, the Living ECK Master is always there to show you the best route to God.

Many who claim to have enlightenment have only had an onrush of emotion, which is mistaken for an actual experience with the Sound and Light of God. This is a precious lifetime. Use it well. No matter what, each day is Soul's golden opportunity to find the Kingdom of God—and enter it in this lifetime. The kingdom of heaven is truly at hand. The secret way to it is through the Audible Sound Current, the Music of God.

In spite of all my experiences in the other worlds, I am still a learner of life. In a real sense, I hope to forever remain that—a child in the wilderness of divine love and mercy.

When you are ready, a way will be opened for you also. In the Light and Sound I salute you, a child of God.

How to Learn More about ECKANKAR

People want to know the secrets of life and death. In response to this need Sri Harold Klemp, today's spiritual leader of ECKANKAR, and Paul Twitchell, its modern-day founder, have written special monthly discourses which reveal the Spiritual Exercises of ECK—to lead Soul in a direct way to God.

Those who wish to study ECKANKAR can receive these special monthly discourses which give clear, simple instructions for the spiritual exercises. The first annual series of discourses is *The ECK Dream Discourses.* Mailed each month, the discourses will offer insight into your dreams and what they mean to you.

The techniques in these discourses, when practiced twenty minutes a day, are likely to prove survival beyond death. Many have used them as a direct route to Self-Realization, where one learns his mission in life. The next stage, God Consciousness, is the joyful state wherein Soul becomes the spiritual traveler, an agent for God. The underlying principle one learns is this: Soul exists because God loves It.

Membership in ECKANKAR includes:

1. Twelve monthly lessons of *The ECK Dream Discourses,* with such titles as: "Dreams—The Bridge to Heaven," "The Dream Master," "How to Interpret Your Dreams," and "Dream Travel to Soul Travel." You may study them alone at home or in a class with others.
2. The *Mystic World,* a quarterly newsletter with a Wisdom Note and articles by the Living ECK Master. In it are also letters and articles from students of ECKANKAR around the world.
3. Special mailings to keep you informed of upcoming ECKANKAR seminars and activities worldwide, new study materials available from ECKANKAR, and more.
4. The opportunity to attend ECK Satsang classes and book discussions with others in your community.
5. Initiation eligibility.
6. Attendance at certain chela meetings at ECK seminars.

How to Find out More

To request membership in ECKANKAR using your credit card (or for a free booklet on membership) call (612) 544-0066 between 8 a.m. and 5 p.m., central time.

Introductory Books on ECKANKAR

Journey of Soul, Mahanta Transcripts, Book 1
Harold Klemp

This collection of talks by ECKANKAR's spiritual leader shows how to apply the unique Spiritual Exercises of ECK—dream exercises, visualizations, and Soul Travel methods—to unlock your natural abilities as Soul. Learn how to hear the little-known Sounds of God and follow Its Light for practical daily guidance and upliftment.

How to Find God, Mahanta Transcripts, Book 2
Harold Klemp

Learn how to recognize and interpret the guidance each of us is *already receiving* from Divine Spirit in day-to-day events—for inner freedom, love, and guidance from God. The author gives spiritual exercises to uplift physical, emotional, mental, and spiritual health as well as a transforming sound called *HU,* which can be sung for inner upliftment.

ECKANKAR—The Key to Secret Worlds
Paul Twitchell

This introduction to Soul Travel features simple, half-hour spiritual exercises to help you become more aware of yourself as Soul—divine, immortal, and free. You'll learn step-by-step how to unravel the secrets of life from a Soul point of view: your unique destiny or purpose in this life; how to make personal contact with the God Force, Spirit; and the hidden causes at work in your everyday life—all using the ancient art of Soul Travel.

The Tiger's Fang, Paul Twitchell

Paul Twitchell's teacher, Rebazar Tarzs, takes him on a journey through vast worlds of Light and Sound, to sit at the feet of the spiritual Masters. Their conversations bring out the secret of how to draw closer to God—and awaken Soul to Its spiritual destiny. Many have used this book, with its vivid descriptions of heavenly worlds and citizens, to begin their own spiritual adventures.

For fastest service, phone (612) 544-0066 weekdays between 8 a.m. and 5 p.m., central time, to request books using your credit card, or look under **ECKANKAR** in your phone book for an ECKANKAR Center near you. Or write: **ECKANKAR, Att: Information, P.O. Box 27300, Minneapolis, MN 55427 U.S.A.**

There May Be an
ECKANKAR Study Group near You

ECKANKAR offers a variety of local and international activities for the spiritual seeker. With hundreds of study groups worldwide, ECKANKAR is near you! Many areas have ECKANKAR Centers where you can browse through the books in a quiet, unpressured environment, talk with others who share an interest in this ancient teaching, and attend beginning discussion classes on how to gain the attributes of Soul: wisdom, power, love, and freedom.

Around the world, ECKANKAR study groups offer special one-day or weekend seminars on the basic teachings of ECKANKAR. Check your phone book under **ECKANKAR**, or call **(612) 544-0066** for membership information and the location of the ECKANKAR Center or study group nearest you. Or write **ECKANKAR, Att: Information, P.O. Box 27300, Minneapolis, MN 55427 U.S.A.**

☐ Please send me information on the nearest ECKANKAR discussion or study group in my area.

☐ I would like an application form to study ECKANKAR further. Please send me more information about the twelve-month ECKANKAR study discourses on dreams.

Please type or print clearly   941

Name _____

Street _____ Apt. # _____

City _____ State/Prov. _____

Zip/Postal Code _____ Country _____

(Our policy: Your name and address are held in strict confidence. We do not rent or sell our mailing lists. Nor will anyone call on you. Our purpose is only to show people the ECK way home to God.)